Belonging

Belonging
The Meaning of Membership

A Report by the Commission on Appraisal
Unitarian Universalist Association

June 2001

Unitarian Universalist Association
Boston

Printed in the United States.

ISBN 1-55896-420-7

10 9 8 7 6 5 4 3 2 1

05 04 03 02 01

We gratefully acknowledge use of the following material:

"Changes" by Caroline Kandler. Reprinted by permission.

"Would You Harbor Me?" Words and music by Ysaye M. Barnwell © 1994, Barnwell's Notes and Publishing. Reprinted by permission.

"How to Kill a Religion" by Meg Muckenhoupt. Reprinted by permision.

"The Epiphany Covenant" reprinted by permission of Epiphany Community Church, Fenton, Michigan.

All Bible quotations are from the New Revised Standard Version.

Contents

Preface   vii

Introduction   xi

The Process of Commitment   1

Theologies of Membership   15

Measures of Membership   39

Creating Thriving Congregations   49

The Challenge of Incarnation   63

Pathways to Growth   77

Investing in Youth and Young Adults   91

Conclusion   103

The Epiphany Covenant   109

UUA Corporate Counsel Opinion on Membership   111

Resources   113

Preface

This report, *Belonging: The Meaning of Membership*, is the tenth report submitted by the Commission on Appraisal of the Unitarian Universalist Association. The bylaws of the UUA provide for the establishment of the Commission:

> The Commission on Appraisal shall consist of nine elected members. A member shall not during the term of office serve as an officer or hold a salaried position in the Association. The Commission on Appraisal shall:
>
> a.   review any function or activity of the Association which in its judgment will benefit from an independent review and report its conclusions to a regular General Assembly;
> b.   study and suggest approaches to issues which may be of concern to the Association; and
> c.   report to a regular General Assembly at least once every four years on the program and accomplishments of the Association (Section 5.8).

Our methodology for this study was eclectic. We held open hearings around the continent during our meetings and at General Assemblies. We held focus groups with specific constituencies within the Association. We sent out questionnaires to selected individuals and congregations, and we held many face-to-face and e-mail to e-mail conversations with people in our movement.

We read the current membership literature, participated in the Memb-L electronic mailing list, and discussed and debated every aspect of the report. We worked not only at our quarterly meetings, but reading, research, and tasks were completed between meetings with the aid of letter, telephone, fax, and e-mail. The project manager and editor carried out the final integration, for which we thank them.

What we submit is a joint effort for which we take joint responsibility. The current commissioners appreciate the work of the former commissioners who contributed to the early stages of the report but whose terms expired before publication: David N. Barus, JD, New York, New York; Rev. George Kimmich Beach, Arlington, Virginia; and Rev. Marjorie Bowens-Wheatley, Boston, Massachusetts. We also thank Rev. John Buehrens for his active interest in our work; as president of the UUA, he is an *ex officio* member of the Commission.

The Commission wishes to thank all those who have assisted in the preparation of this report. Among the individuals who contributed are Rev. Kathleen Allan, David Barus, Roger Butts, Renee-Noelle Felice, Rev. Emily Gage, Susan Grider, Rev. W. Edward Harris, Jacqui James (UUA Anti-Oppression Programs and Resources Director), Rev. Keith Kron (UUA Director, Office of Bisexual, Gay, Lesbian, and Transgender Concerns), Dr. Roger Meyer, Rev. Nurya Love Parish, Rev. Dr. Laurie Proctor, Rev. Tracey Robinson-Harris, Rev. Louis Schwebius, Dr. Norman Shawchuk, Jack Seigel, Rev. Barbara Wells, and Dr. Conrad Wright. In addition, many groups significantly assisted the project. They include persons attending hearings, participants of the Memb-L electronic mailing list of the UUA, participants in camps and conferences who shared their thoughts, respondents to questionnaires on membership, and participants of the focus groups.

Special thanks go to UUA staff members Nancy Lawrence and Peggy Potter-Smith for supporting the Commission in carrying out its duties. The excellent support of our editor, Mary Benard, was essential to the completion of this report, and we also give thanks to the rest of the Publications Department of the UUA (and in particular Joni McDonald) for their expertise in shepherding this report through publication.

The Commission invites comments on this report and on other matters of concern to the Association. Written comments or inquiries may be addressed to the Commission on Appraisal, c/o Unitarian Universalist Association, 25 Beacon Street, Boston, Massachusetts 02108, while e-mail responses may be made to coa@uua.org.

Dr. Janis Sabin Elliot
Portland, Oregon

The Reverend Roberta Finkelstein
Sterling, Virginia

Ms. Joyce T. Gilbert
Rochester, New York

The Reverend Earl K. Holt III
Boston, Massachusetts

Ms. Janice Marie Johnson
New York, New York

The Reverend Lisa Presley
Southfield, Michigan

Dr. Gustave J. Rath
Huntington Beach, California

Mr. Charles B. Redd
Fort Wayne, Indiana

Mr. Arthur J. Ungar
Lafayette, California

Introduction

What is the meaning of membership, or more thoroughly, what are the meanings of membership? What is it that people seek when they affiliate with our congregations? What is it that congregations owe to their membership, and members owe to their congregation? Whom do we include as members of congregations?

These are the questions that came to the Commission on Appraisal as we published our last report, *Interdependence: Renewing Congregational Polity*, in 1997. Yet we realized that these questions were not about polity—the relationship between, among, and within congregations—but rather about the relationships between individuals and congregations. These important questions are worthy of their own report. Consequently, the meaning of membership became the topic of the report we now submit to the General Assembly of the Unitarian Universalist Association.

During the four years of our study (1997–2001), we realized that membership questions are much broader than whom we count for what purposes, and what criteria we establish for legal membership in bylaws. Membership is also, or even more importantly, about how we help the people who come to Unitarian Universalism live out their faith within our congregations, and how the congregations assist them in this endeavor. We realized that we shortchange ourselves, and the world beyond Unitarian Universalism, by focusing only on narrowly construed membership questions such as "How do we do such and such?" We realized that there are multiple resources addressing the how-to's, from first encounter through joining, deepening, and leaving membership. We believe that we can make our most positive impact on the meaning of membership by focusing on what is unique to membership and the meaning of membership within our Unitarian Universalist congregations and how to help our congregations to become more vital, more effective, and more diverse.

What this report is, then, is a study of the questions that we believe are either unique to Unitarian Universalism or to which we as Unitarian Universalists may have unique answers or approaches. We begin by addressing the theological underpinnings of membership, and based on the work of relational and liberation theologians, develop a UU theology of membership. We explore the relationships of the individual to the congregation and the congregation to the individual—what each owes to the other—and how we can best understand these questions. We take what we believe are some of the most appropriate theologies and theories about membership and apply them to our unique position within the religious spectrum, adapting the work of such authors as Loren Mead, Henry Nelson Wieman, Lyle Schaller, and Mary Hunt to our UU history and practices. The result is an understanding of membership that goes beyond numbers and technical requirements, embraces the diversity of practice and people within our movements, and calls our congregations to view membership in a new light.

This new light is that membership is a journey, both for the individual and the congregation. It is not just a technical or legal state, nor only a numerical measurement. It is a process that engages human beings and takes us from a starting place to a new place. By paying careful attention to the paths that provide for this journey, we urge congregations to take into account individual needs for deepening and affirmation. Membership issues do not end when you get a name in "the book"; in fact, this may be when they truly begin.

This report is meant to get Unitarian Universalists thinking. Thinking about their own membership paths, and what they mean. Thinking about the ways their congregations go about meeting the ongoing needs of the membership. Thinking about the values we confer on membership and participation.

And thinking about the multiplicity of difficult issues involved in membership. Some of these difficult issues are numerical and technical, such as the controversy around how to count and report membership to determine Annual Program Fund Fair Share payments. Other issues are philosophical, such as the question of how to embrace people who participate in extra-congregational organizations but haven't found a home in a local congregation. Still others are urgently ethical. These are questions of inclusion and exclusion, of diversity and boundaries.

In looking at these questions, we found Loren Mead's framework, built upon the work of Ted Buckle, to be valuable. Mead suggests four distinct dynamics to church growth: numerical, maturational, organic, and incarnational. By understanding and applying this framework, we believe we can learn much about how to address the tensions inherent in the questions. These tensions are real and can serve either to divide congregations or to prompt them to take creative solutions to their resolution. We hope congregations will do the latter. To aid you, we pose areas to wrestle with, sometimes providing specific questions to help in this endeavor, and other times raising challenges through descriptions of the status quo and what could be. We look at what we think it will take to make Unitarian Universalist congregations and the movement as a whole stronger, as well as provide a more satisfactory, and deeper, experience for individuals who are part of this religious movement.

What this report is not is a how-to manual about membership practices. We did not believe it worthwhile to duplicate the countless wonderful resources that already exist. However we have listed some of our favorites in the Resources at the end of this report for those who have not yet found this literature on their own.

We hope that you will find this report informative, challenging, and transformative of how you and your congregation view the tensions and issues that surround membership. And we hope you join us in trying to achieve the best practices of Unitarian Universalist membership so that all who embrace us philosophically can find a true home within our movement.

Belonging

The Process of Commitment

Why do people join in religious communities? Rev. John Buehrens, president of the Unitarian Universalist Association from 1993 to 2001, notes how central such communities are to the quest for a meaningful life: "To be human is to be religious. To be religious is to make connections. To lead a meaningful life among the many competing forces of the twenty-first century, each of us needs support in making meaningful re-connections to the best in our global heritage, the best in others, and the best in ourselves."[1]

The purpose of this study is to look at the meaning of membership in Unitarian Universalist congregations. Why do people seek out our congregations? Why do they stay? Why do they leave? What about people who grew up in Unitarian Universalist families? Why do they stay? Why do they leave? In order to ensure the health and vitality of our congregations in the twenty-first century, it is important for all of us to consider these questions. We each want a religious home where our own spiritual needs will be met. But we also each need to take a part in creating the kinds of religious communities that attract people who are searching for the same kind of spiritual home we have found— people who have left the religious practices of their childhood, people who grew up unchurched, interfaith couples, and young adults and youth—all of the people who would fill our pews if we would only invite them in.

A study about membership is really a study about evangelism. Not the kind of evangelism that assumes that our religion is better than everybody else's. Not the kind that impels us to change people's minds about their faith journeys. Not

A study about membership is really a study about evangelism.

the imposition of one religious view on unwilling potential converts. Healthy evangelism in Unitarian Universalism is simply—or not so simply—the process of building and sustaining healthy congregations that are welcoming and inclusive, congregations that are staffed and planned to meet one of the most basic of human needs—the need to be religious, to seek meaning, to make connections.

In the course of this study, focus groups were convened in the home congregations of several of the commissioners. Participants in these focus groups were asked to talk about what membership in a Unitarian Universalist congregation meant to each of them. One participant was Mark, a relatively new member of his congregation. He talked about moving into the area from the other side of the country and feeling the need for community. It started in his neighborhood, a small cul-de-sac of new houses. He described the feeling of closeness, the willingness to pitch in. But, he said, "There has been little or no spirituality or discussion of spiritual need. The conversation rarely centers on how we feel about our place in the larger community or our relationship to a higher power." Mark and his wife were looking for a place to engage in meaning making. After joining a local congregation, they found much more. They have joined the choir, taken part in social action projects, assisted with the auction, and facilitated one of the Caring Circles. "As we go forward, we may find it difficult to schedule any additional projects, at least until after the new year. And this is a problem that everyone should have; not enough time to spend with loving, caring people who respect each other, thrive on diversity, and wish the best for the ones with whom they share."

Making connections is the essence of the religious experience. Many people in the focus groups talked about the yearning for community, for friends, for fellowship. For example, Dee had been a self-described solo practitioner of an earth-based religion, but the solitary pursuit left her feeling spiritually empty: "Since becoming a member, I feel more community spirit. There's a great sense of camaraderie among members and friends of this small church, and there are many chances to become involved. I now feel like I belong to a spiritual network.... By working, worshipping, or just plain having fun with others, I get a sense that there's more to religion than just rules and regulations to obediently follow."

The connections that people seek when looking for a religious home are both internal and external. While becoming connected in a "spiritual network" within the congregation is essential, committed membership also means getting connected to the larger community. A healthy congregation will understand its mission to be outward-looking as well as internally focused. In another focus group conducted by Rev. Marjorie Bowens-Wheatley, people active on the membership committee of a large and well-established Unitarian Universalist congregation identified several primary reasons why people stay with their congregation: to be connected to a worshipping community, to feel spiritually grounded (meaning making and internal connections), the congregation's strength in living out its principles and providing opportunities to do social justice work in a structured way (external connections), religious growth and learning—in other words opportunities to "bring their dreams to life" and to share both information and skills with others.[2]

These last items enumerated by the Membership Committee point to the final and most important reason why people become members of our congregations: the need for growth and transformation. Theologian James Luther Adams reminds us that for practitioners of liberal religion, "revelation is continuous."[3] Throughout our lives we humans are learning, growing, changing creatures. Using both reason and intuition, we spend our lives seeking to enlarge our understanding of ourselves and others and the world around us.

The possibility of growth and change, of transformation, is the real basis for participation in a religious community. We have all experienced losses and disappointments, pain and grief. We have been broken by life and need healing. The closest that contemporary Unitarian Universalists may come to a concept of salvation is to offer opportunities for growth and transformation, for becoming more whole. As one of the great ministers of the past century, Rev. A. Powell Davies, memorably put it, "Life is just a chance to grow a soul."[4]

In considering the meanings of membership in Unitarian Universalism, it is important to look not just at the needs people bring to our congregations, but the actual experiences of membership that we offer. Here we move from the general and universal to the particular. What it means to be a member of a church differs depending upon which church it is. In educating our newcomers we commonly focus on religious ideas, and the ways in which our non-doctrinal approach to faith differs from others. But a religion is more than ideas. It is also a set of behaviors, practices, ways of being in community. And these ways of being vary greatly from one congregation to another.

The most obvious example is worship, the unique function of a congregation and usually its most central activity. Styles of worship vary tremendously from congregation to congregation—some relatively formal, others laid back; some predictable in pattern from week to week, others intentionally varied; some elaborate and ceremonial, others plain and simple. What is done and how it is done matter more than the particular ideas that may be articulated on one Sunday or another. The worship expresses, as much by its form as its content, "who we are." Every church evolves its own tradition, even if that tradition is to be untraditional.

What is true of worship is true in subtler ways of all aspects of the congregation's common life. Like individuals, congregations have personalities. Some are more extroverted, others less so. Some are pulpit-centered, even minister-centered; others make high demands for active committee or social participation; still others are focused on music or religious education for children or social action. The point is that every community has its own ways of being. These are not immutable, but they change slowly.

And both in thinking about our congregation, and in introducing it to others, we pay considerably less attention to explicating these characteristics—our way of "being church"—than to, say, the writings of Channing, Emerson, and Parker. But the meaning of membership in a Unitarian Universalist congregation is different from the meaning of membership in, to take a notable example, the Roman Catholic Church, and the differences are deeper than matters of doctrine or even liturgical practice. Congregations are cultures, and these cultures vary widely.

This question of how we convey the culture of our congregations to newcomers is made more complicated by the fact that we are, to a great extent, a convert faith. Our congregations consist overwhelmingly of members from other faith backgrounds. We used to always call them come-outers. Some now refer to them as come-inners. Technically, they would be called converts, a word we tend to avoid and with some justification. The word *conversion* implies a turning about or a turning around, a gradual or sudden shift in perspective. Yet most of those joining our congregations speak less of an experience of conversion than of confirmation: "This is what I always was, but I didn't realize there were others like me, who felt the same way."

Something like this statement is made repeatedly in any gathering of newcomers to one of our congregations. The term *come-outer* referred to the fact that all these people had come out of other congregations and faith traditions. But a closer listening to their stories reveals that most did not, in fact, come out of a Baptist or Presbyterian or Catholic church one day and into one of ours. Rather, in between was some period of time, usually years, in which they lived, as we say, unchurched. Some call this in-between period "nothing." One might also call it secularism. Whatever its name, it is that "nothing" or "secularism" from which they actually came out, or as some now say, came in. If pressed to answer why, most refer to a feeling that "something was missing" in their lives.

This common story has been supplemented in the past decade or so by another slightly different variation, told by those who grew up truly unchurched. They were not raised in even the vaguest institutional religious environment. Their story is different in that it lacks any referent to past church experience, whether embittered or nostalgic or something in between. *Church* is for them a more or less blank slate. Their presence at our doors speaks perhaps to the indelibly religious element in our human nature, and almost certainly to the search for "spirituality," however vaguely defined, which is omnipresent in the current era.

One or another of these stories describes in at least broad outline the experience of some 90 percent of the present membership of our congregations, more than that in many. Overwhelmingly we are what is called a convert faith. The remainder, 10 percent or so, are what are usually called born UUs—or born-inners—the second or later generations of UU families. These percentages have apparently not varied significantly in recent generations, indicating another characteristic of our congregations: Their membership is fluid. In net terms, nearly as many, in some places more, members are exiting by the back door as are coming in by the front. Our failure to retain as adult members a greater percentage of our children has been repeatedly lamented over the years, but there is no evidence of any significant progress in increasing our retention rate.

There is reason to surmise that the increasing mobility of the population affects us more drastically than it does at least some other religious groups. Most of our congregations are small, and there are not that many of them in total. They also differ from one another in a variety of ways. They may possess a common spirit, but they exhibit very different styles. There are differences of theological emphasis and liturgical practice, some as we have said being quite traditional, others more innovative; some are more formal, others less so. We anticipate a range of religious beliefs among our membership and celebrate the theological diversity represented in our congregations, but the consequence is great variability from one congregation to another. Some have strong traditions that may be distinctively Christian, or Theist, or Humanist, for example, which are important to their self-identities. In other congregations the theology may be more eclectic or vary over time depending upon the perspective of the current minister. Since, as we have noted, we are overwhelmingly a convert faith, most of our constituents identify first not as Unitarian Universalists but as members of one particular congregation. And they identify primarily with that congregation's particular expression or style.

In consequence of all these factors, every minister has had the frustration of seeing loyal members of his/her congregation move away to locales where there is either no UU church at all or none that they find congenial based on their prior experiences and expectations. There are of course some denominational loyalists who will make do with whatever they find, but they are relatively few in number.

These factors may also serve to explain the difference that some studies have shown between the substantially larger numbers in the population who identify themselves as Unitarian, Universalist, or Unitarian Universalist and those who are actually members of our congregations. There are apparently two to three times more of the one than the other. In studying this subject we have found it useful to distinguish between and among three categories of those who may be labeled Unitarian Universalist: Identification, Affiliation, and Membership.

UUs by identification are by far the most in number. They include not only those who are presently in some active relationship to a congregation but presumably have had some relationship in the past, significant enough that they still identify themselves religiously by the name, even though they may be

We have found it useful to distinguish between and among three categories of those who may be labeled Unitarian Universalist: Identification, Affiliation, and Membership.

unchurched or even active in another faith tradition. Only a relative handful, apparently, are connected institutionally through the Church of the Larger Fellowship, though perhaps many more could be.

UUs by affiliation include members as well as non-members who are associated with a congregation. Both the Unitarians and the Universalists in earlier periods of our history used a statistic labeled *constituency*. The constituency of every congregation is almost by definition larger, sometimes considerably larger, than its legal membership. It includes, first of all, the children as well as other non-members in member households. For a variety of reasons some individuals who are quite active in their congregations choose not to become members; they pledge, serve on committees, are regular in their attendance at worship. Some will in the course of time become members; others continue in this affiliated status indefinitely for their own reasons. It would be interesting to know whether the number and/or proportion of such individuals varies greatly or little from congregation to congregation and what, if anything, may account for the difference.

UUs by membership are those who have fulfilled the requirements of membership for their congregations. In most of our congregations these requirements are relatively minimal. Usually, signing the membership book or a card of intent suffices. Some congregations have instituted a financial requirement, especially in recent years as the suggested contributions to the UUA Annual Program Fund and Districts have steadily increased.

We propose these three categories of connection as tools for coping positively with the varying levels of commitment and participation that we see in our congregations. It is helpful for us to acknowledge the fact that it is the nature of our faith to have boundaries that are quite permeable. There are certainly many more Unitarian Universalists "in spirit" than there are on the rolls of our congregations, as has been documented in various population research polls. "Are you a Unitarian without knowing it?" was the provocative question of a famously successful advertising campaign conducted by the Layman's League back in the 1950s. Later, others suggested that the important question was not that but rather, "Are you a Unitarian Universalist without showing it?" To show it, they said, meant active membership in a congregation. In hearings that the Commission has held in relation to this study, various individuals and constituencies have raised the question of whether one cannot equally "show it" by participation in non-congregational groups and organizations, including district and continental youth programs, summer camps, and any number of allied and affiliated organizations.

Who is a "member"? Interestingly, this question was addressed in the original Commission of [sic] Appraisal report, published as *Unitarians Face a New Age*, in 1936. Two notable ministers of the period were quoted in that study, both questioning the very value or purpose of counting members, and both

It is the nature of our faith to have boundaries that are quite permeable.

emphasizing our permeable boundaries as a strength. Rev. Dr. Charles E. Park, long-time minister of the First Church in Boston wrote,

> With us church membership is an exceedingly tenuous matter. We are congregations, not corporations. Any fairly regular attendant at one of our churches is virtually a member. Many such have never become technical members, and never will. The result is, our lists of church members tell very little, and their increase or decrease means very little. I think this is as it should be. A real church is a quasi-public institution, to which any member of the community has right of entrance. To make much of membership is to set up a barrier, a low one, doubtless, but still a barrier. What is gained by it? Let the people go out and go in, at will. The important thing is that they find pasture.[5]

Obviously this was written long before the days of Fair Share (per member) contributions to a denominational Annual Program Fund and other practical considerations. But in many respects Dr. Park wrote from a perspective supporting an emphasis on what has been termed membership by affiliation.

The American Unitarian Association did not begin to consistently report church membership in its annual *Year Book* until 1920, and *membership* was somewhat ambiguously defined. Objecting to the practice some fifteen years later, Rev. Maxwell Savage of the First Unitarian Church in Worcester, Massachusetts, published a strongly worded article in the denominational newspaper, the *Christian Register*, declaring,

> Never again let any one among us, at 25 Beacon Street or anywhere else, put forth for publication any figure purporting to be the number of Unitarians there are in this country or any other country. Nobody knows or can know. My belief is that there are far, far more than can be tabulated. But, since nobody can line them up and count them off and brand them, why, oh, why, put out these puny and misguiding figures year by year? Let us stop vying with the denominations of the land. We are not that kind of church. We boast no capital C. As a whole we are not even an organization. We are a movement, an influence, and as such can be most effective.[6]

This statement returns us to the question of what "kind of church" we are. A strong case can be made in defense of Dr. Savage's view, that our greatest impact and importance is not primarily institutional, that we are, as he says, "a movement, an influence."

In response, the Commission of Appraisal cited its "more massive evidence that the Unitarian constituency on the whole is institutionally minded. With many voices it is calling for a leadership which shall found churches and make them succeed in the numerical sense as well in the strength of their more diffused influence."[7] This was the approach taken by the American Unitarian Association and subsequently by the UUA. It is the direction that has been taken by mainline religion in general throughout most of the last half-century and more.

A Broader Definition of Membership

The Commission is suggesting a broader understanding of membership, one that goes beyond our conventional practices and concerns with numbers and technical requirements. Most would agree, we hope, that individuals who fall into the categories of Affiliation and Constituency are also in a meaningful way Unitarian Universalists, while they are generally excluded from our usual definitions of membership. In part this situation has arisen out of a blurring of the distinction between two meanings of the word *church*. In our tradition of congregational polity the word *church* has two distinguishable meanings. These have been described by Conrad Wright, in his important essay, "A Doctrine of the Church for Liberals," in this way:

> In actuality our local religious communities function in two spheres, operating out of two different value systems, which may be in tension with one another. One of these is the sphere of the church, made up of a covenanted body of worshippers. The other is the sphere of the corporation established by law, with power to hold property for religious, educational, and philanthropic purposes. The two are not the same thing, even though the same persons may participate in both, and no formal distinction is made between subscribing to the covenant of the church and signing the bylaws of the legal body corporate.[8]

Historically, the difference between these two "spheres" was recognized institutionally, but this changed over time and awareness of the distinction blurred. The definition of membership in most of our congregations has focused on the secular/corporate meaning of congregation—voting rights, financial support, eligibility to serve as a trustee or represent the congregation at General Assembly—and de-emphasized the religious/communal dimension, the focus of which is the constituency of the "covenanted body of worshippers." Should not this emphasis be somehow reversed?

And is it not in fact reversed in the actual lived life of every congregation? Does not the actual membership of most congregations change almost constantly? It is not a statistic and it is not static; it is not the number of people who may be registered in an official book or reported on a denominational form but a living community that is almost never the same

The Commission is suggesting a broader understanding of membership.

even from week to week. Does not this ever-changing constituency—influenced by birth and death, by affection and alienation, by hurt feelings and reconciliations, by generosity and cold-heartedness, by anger and enthusiasm, by all the exigencies and contingencies of life—make up the real membership of a congregation? A "spiritual body," after all, is literally a breathing body, that is, a living thing. And it is participation in this dynamic, this life, that over time makes one in the deepest theological sense a member and at the same time transforms an agglomeration of individuals into a community.

Membership as Process

In other words, membership is a process. Though there are organizational and institutional needs to define membership cleanly and precisely, the process of membership is in reality a gradual progression from lesser to greater commitment, which neither begins nor ends at the point of formal joining. Thus, for both the individual and the institution the meaning of membership changes over time. Both are continually in process. But it is neither a smooth nor entirely predictable process. *Community* is a happy-sounding word, and it is common for religious liberals to emphasize the ideal of community as a primary reason and purpose for the institution of the church. Such idealism has its place, but building an authentic human community is never easy and only fleetingly happy. The broad appeal of the word itself is suggested by Lyle Schaller's observation that, "the word *community* has now surpassed the word *first* when choosing the name for a new congregation.... In one way or another, nearly every congregation on the North American continent today boasts about the feeling of community the members enjoy. The dream of some is that placing that magical word in the name will both reinforce the sense of community and also attract those seeking a supportive community of believers."[9]

But magic cannot create the warm fuzzy ideal that most people associate with community. Real community can only be built through hard and unglamorous work. Like any effective relationship, it requires commitment. Often these days we hear people say they are seeking a "spiritual community" but want nothing to do with "organized religion." By the former they seem to mean a place that will meet their own religious needs; the latter they seem to associate with a place that will make demands upon them to support the institution's needs. The reality is that you cannot have one without the other, and part of the church's job is to lead people to the discovery of the spiritual truth that it is only by giving that we receive, giving not only our money but ourselves. In other words, only by making a commitment to a community can we hope to build a community. And this commitment consists not of lofty idealisms but of practical realities.

The process of membership is in reality a gradual progression from lesser to greater commitment.

G. Peter Fleck, in the title essay of his book, *The Blessings of Imperfection*, makes direct reference to the lived life of organized religion:

> Well, let's be frank and admit that the church has its aggravations. The eternal and oh-so-necessary concern about finances, the annually recurring problems of balancing a budget, of finding money for repainting the vestibule, repairing the boiler and tuning the organ, the ongoing criticism of the minister's sermons, which are too liberal for some and too orthodox for others, too pedantic for some and too colloquial for others, the endless committee meetings about the Sunday School curriculum and about the propriety of social action, the persistent shortage of tenors in the choir. Who wants it? Who needs it?
>
> The answer to this question is that we...want it, because we need it. The answer is that the church, and I am now speaking of the liberal church, in spite of its shortcomings, the imperfection that characterizes everything made by humans, is better, infinitely better, than no church. Maybe I should not have said "in spite of its shortcomings" but "because of its shortcomings." For isn't it true that in our churches, in these communities of the spirit, we have more resources than outside of our churches to accept each other's imperfections, to reconcile our differences, to forgive and be forgiven, to comfort and to be comforted, to love and to be loved? Isn't that what the church is all about—because it is what life is all about?[10]

At the very least it is what religious community is all about. Fleck writes as what he is, a highly committed layperson with a deep love of the church. How has he learned such loyalty? By an idealism grounded in realism, by a continuing commitment to what the church could be, sufficient to transcend its all-too-human realities, its pettiness, and failures to live up to its own ideals. Undoubtedly, in a long life of churchgoing, he had lived through much disillusionment. And remarkably enough, we have noted that disillusionment plays a key part in the process of membership, in the process engendering loyalty and commitment.

First Disillusionment and Religious Community

Dietrich Bonhoeffer, in a book on Christian fellowship entitled *Life Together*, has addressed this subject theologically. He writes, "Only that fellowship which faces such Disillusionment, with all its unhappy and ugly aspects, begins to be what it should be in God's sight, begins to grasp in faith the promise that is given to it. The sooner this shock of disillusionment comes to an individual and to a community the better for both." He calls the idealization of community a "human wish dream" that "is a hindrance to genuine community and must be banished if genuine community is to survive."[11]

A commitment to building real religious community together is one of the significant meanings of church membership. How one reacts to one's first disillusionment (and all the other disappointments that eventually follow) is an indicator and test of that commitment. Adversity is an aspect of every process of growth. To paraphrase Bonhoeffer only slightly, "Those who love their dreams of community more than the community itself become destroyers of the latter, even though their personal intentions may be ever so honest and earnest and sacrificial."

One of the continuing challenges for liberalism is its inability to inspire and engender institutional commitments, transcendent of the concerns and interest of a given time or place. Albert Einstein's wife was once asked if she understood the theory of relativity. She replied, "No, but I know my husband, and I know he can be trusted." Most Unitarian Universalists are not quite so trusting. Liberalism necessarily carries with it an edge of suspicion. But you have to be trusting to be disillusioned, and surprising as it may seem, such disillusionment plays a crucial role in developing loyalties and commitments.

This disillusionment takes place at the institutional level as well as the personal. This is almost inevitable in the course of one's relationship to a congregation. The congregation that is supposed to be a loving community is sometimes beset with conflicts. The congregation that is supposed to be affirming and gentle can become narrow and unfeeling. Decisions can be made with which we disagree. People can become disagreeable. These are the same problems the apostle Paul dealt with almost two thousand years ago in establishing the first Christian communities. The church is a human institution and it can become all-too-human. When such difficulties arise some walk away, others step back. But fortunately there are also those who remain steadfast through these times of disillusionment, whose loyalty grows beyond it. They are not better or worse than the others, just different. Out of their disillusionment grows a loyalty less to the institution and more to the values and ideals that the institution seeks to serve and embody. It recognizes that institutional as well as personal failure is virtually inevitable. This is loyalty of a high order. It requires extraordinary patience, tolerance, and the capacity to forgive. These are spiritual gifts, learned in real community.

Those who have gained these capacities, these gifts, are in the deepest sense members: people who are committed for the long haul, those who have a loyalty not just to what the church is but what it could be, what it can become through their persistence and with their assistance. They are committed in other words, not so much to the institution as to the values and ideals it exists to promote and uphold—even in its periods of failure to do so. They are patient with brash young ministers and tolerant of plodding older ones. They

One of the continuing challenges for liberalism is its inability to inspire and engender institutional commitments.

are cheerleaders in the good times and steady supporters through the bad. They keep perspective, they take a longer view.

Henry Nelson Wieman, a Unitarian and process theologian, wrote of religion and faith as being not simply ultimate concern but ultimate commitment. Inevitably in our lives we commit ourselves to something, whether worthy or not. The direction and intensity of our loyalties give shape and meaning to our lives.

Loyalties, commitments, covenants, the promises we make to one another: These are the things that relate to the deepest meanings of membership. They tell us what we belong to. And by doing that they tell us who we are.

We have made some assumptions about what brings people to our congregations and what invites a significant membership commitment. From these assumptions we can also identify the characteristics of a congregation that will best meet those needs and elicit that commitment. First of all, a healthy congregation will provide worship services and other programs that encourage the search for meaning. Our UUA Statement of Principles and Purposes calls for our congregations to be places where this search can take place: "We, the member congregations of the Unitarian Universalist Association, covenant to affirm and promote...acceptance of one another and encouragement to spiritual growth in our congregations; a free and responsible search for truth and meaning...." The local congregation can be envisioned as a laboratory where people bring their life experiences, responses, feelings, hopes, and dreams. The great experiment is to put all of that together in a form that creates meaning, gives definition to each person, and allows each person to expand his/her perspective and to continually seek and occasionally find transformation.

Rev. George K. Beach, in a 1999 Minns Lecture, uses a story from James Luther Adams that illustrates this understanding that the purpose of the church is transformation:

> In the First Unitarian Church of Chicago we started a program some of us called "aggressive love" to try to desegregate that Gothic cathedral. We had two members of the Board objecting. Unitarianism has no creed, they said, and we were making desegregation a creed. It was a gentle but firm disagreement and a couple of us kept pressing. "Well, what do you say is the purpose of this church?" we asked, and we kept it up until about 1:30 in the morning. We were all worn out, when finally this man made one of the great statements, for my money, in the history of religion. "OK, Jim. The purpose of this church...well, the purpose of this church is to get hold of people like me and change them!"[12]

Beach then goes on to say, "The purpose of the church is also to expose us to perspectives that fall outside our commonly circumscribed, self-protected existences, in order that we shall have the opportunity to read the signs of the times and to change."[13]

Our congregations need to be places where connections can be made, networks that connect people to each other in meaningful ways. In contemporary American culture, the dislocations of traditional sources of rootedness are well known: the breakdown of the close-by extended family, the suburban sprawl replacing local neighborhoods, the mall replacing the corner store. No wonder individualism is rampant! People seek out a congregation because they need a place to belong—to be rooted, to work out questions of value and meaning, to have a spiritual life.

People seek out a congregation because they need a place to belong.

The congregation that understands its purpose in terms of offering people a place to grow and change and to make connections will also be a congregation that understands itself to be an organic entity that also grows and experiences transformation. George K. Beach asserts, "People do not 'join' a covenanted community; rather they constitute it; there is no 'it' without them and each time new folks join, the whole is literally reconstituted."[14] A member of a local congregation opined that he understood membership in terms of how strongly one can influence the destiny of the group. If people enter into the membership experience with the expectation that change will be the result, the structure of our congregations needs to be one that allows for flexibility and change. If in fact we understand the congregation to be reconstituted with the addition of each new member, then it can be no other way. Every person brings a different set of experiences and expectations and ways of doing things to the mix. The result will always be different, surprising, and vital.

A vital, growing, changing congregation is bound to look outward as well as inward. In addition to supporting the spiritual growth and deepening faith of individual members, it will always be asking the question about how it fits into the larger community. By words and deeds that are visible and audible, a healthy congregation shows people what Unitarian Universalism is at its best. You might say that this is the most powerful form of evangelism: demonstrating the possibilities that liberal religion offers simply by being the way we are in the world.

Notes

1. John A. Buehrens, "Preface" in *The Unitarian Universalist Pocket Guide*, 3rd ed., edited by John A. Buehrens (Boston: Skinner House Books, 1999), x.
2. Marjorie Bowens-Wheatley, Case Study (Commission on Appraisal, 1998), 6.
3. James Luther Adams, *On Being Human Religiously*, 2nd ed. (1976; reprint, Boston: Skinner House Books, 1986), 12.
4. A. Powell Davies as quoted in Buehrens, op. cit., x.

5. Commission of Appraisal, *Unitarians Face a New Age* (Boston: American Unitarian Association, 1936), 229.

6. Ibid., 230.

7. Ibid.

8. Conrad Wright, *Walking Together: Polity and Participation in UU Churches* (Boston: Unitarian Universalist Historical Society, 1998), 13.

9. Schaller, Lyle. *The Seven-Day-a-Week Church* (Nashville, TN: Abingdon Press, 1992), 27.

10. G. Peter Fleck. *The Blessings of Imperfection: Reflections on the Mystery of Everyday Life* (Boston: Beacon Press, 1987), 8.

11. Dietrich Bonhoeffer, *Life Together* (San Francisco: Harper, 1954), 27.

12. James Luther Adams as quoted in George Kimmich Beach, "The Parables of James Luther Adams," in *The Minns Lectures, 1999* (Boston: Unitarian Universalist Association, 1999), 63.

13. George Kimmich Beach, "The Parables of James Luther Adams," in *The Minns Lectures, 1999* (Boston: Unitarian Universalist Association, 1999), 63.

14. Ibid., 55.

Theologies of Membership

What is a member? Perusing the definitions in numerous dictionaries yields a wide variety of answers. One in particular, from an older edition of *Webster's Dictionary*, seems particularly relevant. This edition defines a member as "...one who forms part of a metaphysical or metaphorical body." This is clearly a reference to the imagery found in I Corinthians 12:12.[1] When UUA President John Buehrens met with the Commission on Appraisal in the course of our work on this report, he urged us, as part of our membership study, to look at this text. This passage is so often quoted in the literature about church membership that it is hard to ignore. How could this image be helpful to Unitarian Universalists, given its endurance and power?

The image is powerful and enduring because it was carefully drawn out of several powerful and enduring cultural contexts. The first was the idea of being a covenanted people—the basic message of the Hebrew Bible. The early Christian community held on to that idea of being in covenant—they understood themselves to be people in covenant with the same God who had been in covenant with their Abrahamic ancestors. They understood Jesus to be the mediator of a new covenant, but that new covenant was in continuity with the old. The word *covenant* is still relevant to our contemporary understanding of membership in the liberal church. In fact, one of the purposes of the Unitarian Universalist Association's strategic planning process, called *Fulfilling the Promise*, is to encourage a process of recovenanting—both in local congregations and among the congregations that together constitute the Association. Individual

Unitarian Universalists and congregations are being challenged to answer questions such as: How shall we treat each other? What are we willing to promise each other? What does it mean to be "We, the member congregations"?[2]

The author of I Corinthians, presumably Paul of Tarsus, also drew on the understanding of citizenship in the Greco-Roman world in offering his body of Christ metaphor. Being part of a larger whole—an individual contributing to the workings of a larger organization—echoed the Hellenistic ideal of a democracy in which every citizen participated. That ideal of participatory democracy is imbedded in the heart of our Unitarian Universalist Principles in the words, "...the use of the democratic process in our congregations and in society at large...."

Further, Roman citizens understood themselves to be Romans no matter where in the world they found themselves. Being a Roman bestowed an identity. When Paul reminded those Corinthian adherents that they were, by their baptism, brought into one body, he was reminding them that their identity as Christians was as profound as their identity as Romans. No matter where they went or what happened to them, they would always be Christians. Would that our identification as Unitarian Universalists bestowed such a profound sense of religious identity!

This kind of deep identification with our faith tradition would, perhaps, keep our young people committed to Unitarian Universalism after graduating from our religious education programs. It would change the membership practices in our local congregations so that they reflected the depth of love and care that we feel for them. No more "easy in, easy out" attitude! A meaningful religious identity is a reflection of a meaningful path to membership. And a meaningful path to membership can only be laid by people who have committed to our congregations; people who have not only "signed the book" but have experienced an increasing spiritual depth. Identity, spirituality, and sense of commitment all depend on each other to develop. Whether a Christian in the Roman Empire or a Unitarian Universalist in contemporary Western culture, a religious identity both bestows something upon and asks something of one.

Being a member of a community of faith is what makes the meaning of one's religious identity come alive.

But just as the Roman citizen self-identified as a Roman, he/she was a member of a local colony—a subset of the empire.[3] One needed to be part of a local community in order to live out one's identity. So too, affiliation with a local church was important to maintaining the meaning of the Christian identity. Just claiming the label *Christian* did not bestow that profound identity. Being a member of a community of faith is what makes the meaning of one's religious identity come alive. Not just by faith, but by affiliation is one saved! And so it is with Unitarian Universalism. We are, by historical tradition, a strongly congregational faith. Primary religious affiliation, like the power of decision making, is located primarily in the local congregation. While many people claim to be Unitarian Universalists without affiliating with a Unitarian

Universalist congregation, a more profound identity develops in the context of the local congregation.

It is important to understand that Chapter 12 in I Corinthians begins by talking about spiritual gifts.[4] Paul urges his followers to recognize the many and varied spiritual gifts in the Christian community and to welcome and make use of all of them. He then goes on to use a metaphor of the body to describe the church. All are brought together by baptism and together make up one spiritual body. No one organ or part is more important than another; all are essential to the healthy functioning of the whole. In fact, the more frail parts are the most indispensable; the most unseemly are given the most honor: "If one member suffers, they all suffer together with it; if one member is honored, all rejoice together with it. Now you are the body of Christ and individually members of it" (I Cor. 12: 26-27).

The emphasis of this text is on building a fellowship based on equality, unity, and mutuality.[5] The church that Paul urges the Corinthians toward is one in which individual persons become part of something greater. It is not a place one would join simply in order to "find one's self." A family shopping for the church with the most benefits would not find this one to their liking. As Bernard Jones puts it, "It is clear that the church was not an organization that an individual went along to join as he might make an application to join a golf club. It was an 'ecclesia'—a group of people called . . ."[6] A *calling* implies the expectation of a serious and transforming relationship. People called to membership take that membership seriously. A church built on equality, unity, and mutuality will appeal to those who are looking for a repository for their particular gifts and talents, who are looking for a place to grow beyond their own particular perspectives. It is also a church that will appeal to people who are looking for a way to live out their faith in the larger community. It is a church that celebrates the whole that is so much more than the sum of the parts, that welcomes and encourages all comers to be part of an organic entity that stretches well beyond the vision or intent of any one individual leader. It is a church where "I can take care of myself" is replaced by "We can and will take care of each other."

It is almost a cliché that individualism and personal entitlement have come close to crippling American democracy in general and Unitarian Universalism in particular. What Robert Bellah calls *ontological individualism* has led to a loss of a collective understanding of the common good at many levels from the halls of Congress to the annual meetings of Unitarian Universalist congregations. George Rupp claims that in this atmosphere, communities of faith have an obligation to stand in opposition to a narrow focus on individual fulfillment:

> Over against this orientation, communities of faith must oppose any and every view that begins uncritically with separate selves and then almost unavoidably becomes preoccupied with achieving satisfaction for the self,

"I can take care of myself" is replaced by "We can and will take care of each other."

including satisfying relationships as simply a means to this end. Over against this orientation, communities of faith must remind us all that we do not begin as separate entities, which then somehow must become connected.

Rupp rather elegantly and forcefully reminds us of the image that Paul gave to the Corinthians: "Instead, we are all members of a common body—a body that is broken, even fragmented, but that is also an expression of the finally all-inclusive divine-human community in which we live and love and have our being."[7]

So if I Corinthians 12 has something to say to contemporary Unitarian Universalists about the meaning of membership, what exactly is it? It is that membership in a Unitarian Universalist congregation can be a profound experience—an experience that brings us into covenant with other people who, though diverse in their personal experiences and needs, all seek one thing in common: wholeness. The experience of membership offers to individuals the opportunity to become more whole, more committed to each other and to that which is of ultimate worth, more grounded, more profoundly human, and more aware of the gift of community. The experience of membership both affirms inherent personal worth and confers a new and expanded sense of worth as a member of a local congregation and as a Unitarian Universalist.

Becoming a member of the body of Unitarian Universalism is an opportunity to find honor, affirmation, freedom, commitment, and salvation. Understand salvation not as an entry pass into another world at death, but as the recognition that right here we have an opportunity to be more than we currently are, to become complete, to find wholeness, health, shalom.

A relevant theology of membership will understand membership as an organic and ongoing process.

The ancient biblical metaphor for membership contained in I Corinthians informs concepts learned from the very contemporary literature of systems theory and organizational development. A relevant theology of membership based on a systems view will understand membership as an organic and ongoing process. People (members and potential members) seek out the particular relationship that is membership in a particular local congregation. Each individual brings to this process certain needs, expectations, and personal history; the congregation also carries its history and expectations into every new relationship. Understanding the process means understanding what happens to that organic whole (the congregation) as it expands and contracts in order to accommodate the dynamic parts (members) that make it up. In developing a theology of membership for Unitarian Universalism, we propose and attempt to answer several questions.

First consider the question of *identity*. What is it that an individual assents to in becoming a member? How is each of us changed by our experience of membership in a local congregation? Just as importantly, how is the congregation changed? And how does it remain the same—what is it about the church that is consistent, even immutable? Since membership in the local congregation is built on relationships, a theology of membership will be a relational theology.

The next question is one of *formation*. If membership is an ongoing process, what is it that I am becoming or moving toward as my journey into membership progresses? What do I learn? What do I give and get? What structures are provided to ensure what Loren Mead calls the maturational growth of the congregation?[8]

Finally there is the question of *worship and ritual*. How does the church take note of and celebrate the identifiable moments when identity changes, when milestones are reached in the process of formation? There are the obvious celebrations such as child dedications and new member recognition ceremonies. What about installation of officers? Affirmation of lay ministries? We note ritually the milestones in our faith journeys in many different ways. Youth Sunday is, in many congregations, an opportunity for our adolescents to make powerful statements about their faith and their sense of commitment. Congregations that offer a Coming of Age program to their youth often give youth an opportunity to conduct worship services in which they share their adolescent faith journeys. Likewise, many Unitarian Universalist summer camps and conferences, as well as district conferences and the General Assembly, offer a bridging ceremony that welcomes older youth into the young adult community. Perhaps some congregations also follow this practice. We need to offer more such opportunities for people of all ages to reflect on their faith journeys and their sense of connection to the congregation.

Unitarian Universalist minister Linda Olson-Peebles offers a definition of ritual that is important to our understanding of worship. "Ritual," she says, "is an act or event which carries with it memory and association beyond the event itself." Rituals remind us that there is more to this life than just what we bring to it.[9] John Burkhart, author of several preaching and worship texts, adds this to our understanding: "Rituals are symbolic activities that speak for themselves while pointing beyond themselves. They are expressive [for example, when we light a chalice at the beginning of a service, we understand that the chalice is more than just a candle—it is a reminder of our history, of our connections to other Unitarian Universalists]. Worship changes people."[10]

A theology of membership will include questions of identity, formation, and worship practices. It should offer a vision of what life in the local Unitarian Universalist congregation can be—a transcendent vision that acknowledges the importance of the day-to-day work of the church but also pulls people past issues of money and status into the realm of the ultimate. It should organize our approach to faith, practice, and experience in the local congregation. George Rupp, in his study of the nature of commitment in contemporary religious communities, reminds us that an adequate theology must be both descriptive and prescriptive.[11] That is, it must take into account the whole spectrum of realities it is attempting to address, and it must also enable people to see the possibilities and ideas inherent in their communities of faith.

It is important to emphasize that the impetus for an individual to seek membership in a local congregation is still a subjective experience, not a theoretical construct. As we develop our theology of membership, our prescription will be to move from a focus on the individual to a focus on the organic whole. But we must always remember that each person becomes part of that whole through his/her individual lens. This assumption resonates with the first Source in our Unitarian Universalist Statement of Principles and Purposes, a legacy from our Transcendentalist ancestors.[12] It also resonates with Henry Nelson Wieman's contention that theology must be empirical, by which he means that theological thinking begins with the evidence we gather with our own senses: "We can have no spiritual experience which does not include sense experience, because the living organism is always sensing.... Every power of cognition, every power or appreciation, devotion, love and aspiration requires sense experience in its beginning and in its development."[13]

We cannot create a theology (or a church) that is completely new. All we can do is gather our various experiences of life and try to put together a community that responds to the questions, issues, and needs that those experiences raise. This process will inevitably raise more questions and bring forth different issues. A healthy congregation is an organic entity; it will experience growth and change as will the individuals who constitute it.

A healthy congregation will experience growth and change as will the individuals who constitute it.

As Unitarian Universalists we know as well as anybody that our church, our faith, is the product of human reason and imagination. We also know that our congregations are voluntary associations. They were created by free people exercising their free will and making the decision to come together for worship, fellowship, and service. This is the legacy of our ancestors in the Radical Reformation. Those brave people died for their belief that religion should be a matter of choice. Rev. Dr. Rebecca Parker, president of the Starr King School for the Ministry, reminds us that there are some relationships we are born into, and others that we choose voluntarily. All those relationships bring benefits and confer obligations. Our theology of membership will address both the benefits and the obligations of our freely chosen religious association.

Our theology will reflect our history and our widely divergent contemporary viewpoints. We don't have an authoritative book, creed, or priestly class to give credence to our corporate body. All we have is ourselves and each other, and the many people who chose our particular path before us. George Rupp says that one of the problems faced by the contemporary church in general is coming to terms with the realization that the symbolic universe of religious communities is "a creation of collective human insight and imagination"[14] as opposed to something that emerged directly from the hand or mouth of God. It may be easier for us to live with that realization than it is for some other religious faiths. But even that recognition requires a willingness to honor the collective, and to give up our assumption that any one personal, subjective human experience is sufficient basis for a full religious life. We move from the individual to the collective, seeking wholeness and completeness.

So we gather our experiences, and we create our congregations. We acknowledge that what we create is not completely new, though it may differ radically from other communities of faith. But just as we build on a diverse spectrum of traditions and experiences, we also build on the thinking of theologians from a wide variety of traditions. The Commission believes that there are two major threads of contemporary theological thinking that can inform our theology of membership: relational theologies and liberation theology.

Two major threads of contemporary theological thinking can inform our theology of membership: relational theologies and liberation theology.

Relational Theologies

Relational theologies are ways to understand how it is possible to elevate human relationships to the level of ultimate worth and meaning, to make real John Buehrens's assertion that Unitarian Universalism is a movement that "*embodies* a reverent and respectful pluralism" (emphasis ours). One of the most important things we learned from the focus groups we convened in the research phase of this report is that for many people, the experience of fellowship, of connection to other people, was the single most important factor in evaluating the meaning of their membership. Interpersonal relationships make going to church a more significant experience. We therefore wanted to develop a theological framework that took this into account; a theology of human relationships. Two of the most important theologians in this area of relational theology are Mary Hunt and Henry Nelson Wieman.

Although Hunt and Wieman are in many ways light-years apart, they have in common some basic assumptions that are particularly relevant to the work of articulating a theology of membership for Unitarian Universalism. First of all, both assume that in some way, individuals encounter the holy in intentional, nurturing relationships. Both authors are humanistic, not in the sense that they necessarily reject the possibility of a deity, but in the sense that they believe in the centrality of human experience. Rev. Harold Rosen offers this definition of humanistic theology: "Wieman's thought is humanistic, as opposed to transcendentalist on one hand, or mechanistic on the other. He repeatedly emphasizes how all evidence to date supports the view that, for better or for worse, human beings are the agents within whom the greatest value-appreciation has been released into the known universe."[15]

Finally, relational theologies are transformative, generative, and directed toward the creation of community. This means that individuals who enter into particular relationships can expect to be changed by these relationships, to become more caring, more concerned with the well-being of people around them, and more able and willing to effect change.

In spite of what they have in common, the thought and the models proposed by Hunt and Wieman are radically different from each other; so much so that they cannot be presented together.

Henry Nelson Wieman is a process thinker; his work is based on the assumptions of process philosophy developed by Alfred North Whitehead. James Luther Adams has described Whitehead as a thinker whose

> primary concern is to catch and communicate a religious vision of the meaning of life, indeed to grasp and communicate a vision of greatness. This vision, he is convinced, has to do with something more than the life of the individual. In short...it is concerned with what individuals and groups do with their solitariness in relationship—with their togetherness.[16]

Wieman describes religion as "man's [sic] attempt to realize the highest good, through coming into harmonious relations with some reality greater than himself, which commands his reverence and loyal service."[17]

Although Wieman is humanistic in his understanding of human nature and its place in the universe, he is also theistic in that he believes that there is something other than humanity that is worthy of our ultimate commitment. God, in process theology, is not understood to be a Being, but a Process. Wieman says, "God is the growth which springs anew when old forms perish."[18] Rosen further elaborates that "God, then, is the generative source of all constructive values."[19]

Wieman proposes a four-step process through which creative interchange happens. Keep in mind that this process is not linear but cyclical. Step one is called *emergent perspectives*. In this step, individuals reflect on their own life experiences. They do this not in isolation, but in a group setting. Each person then communicates some of what he/she has concluded to others. When people talk to each other about their lives—what has happened, what has been important, what has been felt most deeply—they learn to attach meaning to experience. The second step is *progressive integration*. In this step, the exchange of meanings from step one leads each person to enrich his/her own thoughts and feelings with the meanings of others. This step, unlike the first, is more likely to happen in solitude.

The third step is called *expanding appreciation*. During this step the shared values are integrated into one's way of living, and as a result his/her world expands—the range of experiences that he/she can understand and analyze is larger. Wieman describes it as "a range and variety of events, a richness of quality, and a reach of ideal possibility which were not there prior to this transformation."[20] Though the subject for reflection is one's own life, the process requires the presence and encouragement of other people. The group allows

When people talk to each other about their lives, they learn to attach meaning to experience.

each person to become more than any of them could have been while struggling alone.

Wieman calls the final step in the creative interchange *growing community*: "If you and I have expanded our appreciable worlds as individuals, then the relations we have with our respective communities will also prove creatively transforming, such that they will grow in healthy, non-competitive ways."[21] This is the action step and it points the way toward justice, care of others, and deepening of relational bonds.

The great value in Wieman's work is that it gives us a way to make our human relationships worthy of our ultimate commitment. In thinking about a theology of membership, it is essential to be able to identify the very real human-to-human relationships as the basic reality of people's experience of belonging to a congregation. If we can use language that elevates these relationships to the level of the holy—that which is of ultimate worth—we can begin to explore membership as an experience that has deep and enduring value.

Mary Hunt is a contemporary feminist theologian associated with the Women's Alliance for Theology and Ritual. Her basic contention is that friendship is a relationship that reveals what is of ultimate worth to us. Friendship is a voluntary association freely entered into by two or more persons. It reflects human choice; the nature of the relationship shows intentionality. She has created a model for the theological study of friendship that has four elements: love, power, embodiment, and spirituality. The model is dynamic and circular, like Wieman's process of creative interchange. When these four elements work in harmony the friendship is generative. This means that the process generates something new "for both persons and for the larger community of which they are a part. Generativity is the hallmark of friendship."[22]

Love is the intention to recognize the drive in relationships towards unity and community. Love is a commitment to deepen bonds between persons without losing individuality. Love is the power that allows for unity in diversity, that illusive goal we are always reaching for. By *power*, Hunt means the ability of individuals to make choices. Power is individual and personal. It is also social and structural. In a congregation built on a theology of friendship, justice-seeking friends exercise their personal power in order to make changes in structural power. *Embodiment* is included in the model to acknowledge the fact that all of our reactions and relationships are mediated by our physical bodies. As the Humanist psychologist Abraham Maslow teaches us, lack of proper nutrition, rest, health care, pleasure, and work impinges on our ability to enter into community. Communities created out of the power and love of friendship encourage their members toward "healthy, integrated embodiment."[23] This concept of embodiment reflects an understanding of the worth of every individual, and echoes Buehrens's description of Unitarian Universalism.

We can use language that elevates these relationships to the level of the holy to explore membership as an experience that has deep and enduring value.

Spirituality is defined not as a private, ethereal quality but as an intentional process of making choices that affect self and community. Hunt believes that concern for meaning and value is ultimately expressed in very concrete ways—in ways that affect the quality of life for self and community. Spirituality is attentiveness, focus, awareness of how our behavior and choices affect the people around us.

Hunt's model offers us another way to use covenantal language without invoking the traditional God image of the traditional covenant. She elevates aspects of human relatedness to the realm of the holy. Love, power, embodiment, and spirituality become matters of ultimate concern and commitment.

Both Hunt and Wieman offer us a theological basis for talking about human relationships as matters of ultimate worth. If we are to deepen the meaning of membership in our congregations, it is essential that we acknowledge that what we hold sacred is the community that is created when we come together. Relational theologies can help us to invoke the holy when we talk about our ways of being together.

Liberation Theology

Personal spiritual growth and social transformation are equally important.

Being together in a meaningful way is profoundly important, but it is not a sufficient reason for the existence of the liberal church. If membership were based only on face-to-face relationships, the church would lose its power to act as an agent of transformation. Personal spiritual growth and social transformation are equally important, and our congregations, in order to make membership meaningful, must find ways to actualize these ideals. We therefore turn to the theories of liberation theology to elucidate these outward-looking aspects of membership.

The most basic definition of liberation theology would probably be "reflective praxis." That is, a group of people think critically about their life experiences, their cultural context, their history, and their faith stance. They then take action based on the results of that reflection. This is not a linear process; it is cyclical. Reflection and praxis are part of an ongoing process of engaging with the world. This process would allow Unitarian Universalists to realize more fully our dream of being a truly diverse and inclusive movement. It engages human reason, makes room for a wide variety of experiences and opinions, and empowers all people to the work of making sense of their own unique lives.

Several concepts that all liberation theologies hold in common are important for us. The first is that theology done from a liberation perspective is always contextual. This means that it is rooted in the particularities of a given time and place; it emerges out of the real-life experience of the people engaged in the process. This is what makes it possible for people who are relatively uneducated to "do" theology. Although it is rooted in particularities, it is related to the universal and points toward the development of meaning. Theologian James Cone says, "I firmly believe that the issues to which theology addresses itself should be those that emerge out of life in a society as persons seek to achieve meaning in a dehumanized world."[24]

Any Unitarian Universalist who has taken the *Building Your Own Theology* curriculum will be familiar with the liberationist understanding of the nature of theological inquiry. Rev. Dr. Richard Gilbert says in that curriculum, "I continue to maintain that theology comes out of the tough and tender experiences of life: first comes the experience (religion) and then the reflection on that experience (theology)."[25]

Second, liberation theology is an engaged theology. It is in dialogue with the culture; it seeks to understand the history of a people in terms of their experiences of oppression and freedom, exploitation and justice. "Do we believe," asks Unitarian Universalist theologian Dr. Thandeka, "that simply to think about an issue is the same as to live in a way which exemplifies our concern for the issue?"[26] This question, addressed specifically to Unitarian Universalists, nudges us rather urgently toward engagement.

Third, liberation theology is always hopeful. History is mined in order to understand not just what has happened but what could have been and what still could be. It is, in essence, the use of history to project a more hopeful future, what mujerista theologian Ada Maria Isasi-Diaz calls "the preferred future as a source of hope."[27] Unitarian Universalism has always been a hopeful faith—sometimes accused of unfounded optimism. However, if our faith in the future comes not from ignoring the pain of the present but from transforming it through a careful process of reflection and action, there is, as in the tile of Rev. Dr. Frederick Muir's book, a reason to hope. As liberation theologian Gustavo Gutierrez writes, "The commitment to the creation of a just society, and, ultimately, a new humanity, presupposes confidence in the future."[28]

Fourth, the basic process of liberation theology is critical reflection. This is the place where we believe that exciting work could be done in Unitarian Universalist congregations. We already have a tradition of honoring the use of reason. We have too often assumed that only well-educated, well-read people could "do" Unitarian Universalist theology. However, Rev. Lucy Hitchcock, in a conversation with the Commission on Appraisal, reminded us that poor people, uneducated people, can "be thoughtful about the world."

Hitchcock referred to the work of Paolo Freire in this regard. Freire has done groundbreaking work in Brazil with uneducated and illiterate populations. His purpose is to move them from "naïve awareness to critical awareness."[29] His book *Pedagogy For The Oppressed* has applications in this country as well. It is cited in a leadership training manual produced by Youthbuild USA, which works with inner-city American youth. YouthBuild incorporates his ideas into its youth organizing by building basic literacy and public speaking skills into all programming.

This is an exciting avenue for Unitarian Universalists to pursue in our quest to make our congregations more diverse. Using a liberation process, we could open up our process of theology building so that it recognizes and welcomes the participation of people whom we have previously thought of as not well-read or well-educated enough. It would be, first of all, a matter of educating ourselves about the fact that critical reflection on lived experience is not the exclusive business of the intellectual elite or the well-educated. Then, together with our new partners in theology, we could all become what Gutierrez calls the organic intellectuals, that is, "theologians personally and vitally engaged in historical realities."[30]

The fifth characteristic of liberation theology is that it is always a justice-seeking process. Liberation theologies have all arisen out of the experience of oppression—economic, social, and racial/ethnic. For each particular strand of liberation theology, the basic question is always, "What does this painful experience mean, given the promises that our faith tells us God has made?" In other words, where is God in the process of oppression? The answer, in various ways, is that God clearly expresses a preferential option for the poor. The preferential option for the poor has been a part of biblical interpretation for millennia. The prophets of the Hebrew scriptures railed against economic injustice. Jesus continually urged his followers to shed their worldly possessions and focus on acts of justice and of healing. Rev. Richard Gilbert credits Thomas Aquinas with best articulating the theological basis for this "preferential option" in his discussion of distributive justice.[31] When the Bible is read through the lens of this preferential option, a commitment to justice is an inevitable result.

Justice seeking is the praxis piece of the cycle. Isasi-Diaz explains, "In mujerista theology, praxis is critical reflective action based on an analysis of historical reality perceived through the lens of an option for a commitment to liberation."[32] The result of a belief that God has a preferential option for the poor is not to sit around waiting for God to act on that preference. Belief in the preferential option is, instead, the inspiration for people to act.

Isasi-Diaz talks extensively about the development of moral agency in Hispanic women. Moral agency means making your own lived experience available to others; it allows people to become self-determining. In mujerista theology, moral agency is generative; that is, to become a moral agent means to take on increased responsibility for and care for the community. It is not about individual self-actualization but about changing the experience of the whole community. "Life," she says, "is life if it is linked to others."[33]

While mujerista theology comes out of a theistic tradition, its theme of moral agency is echoed in the work of Unitarian Universalist theologian William R. Jones, a firm Humanist. Jones urges us to believe in "the functional ultimacy of humanity."[34] In other words, whether or not you believe there is a God, you had better act as though a better world is up to you!

And this leads to the sixth and final aspect of liberation theology—it is Humanist. Not in the contemporary understanding of Humanist in opposition to theist—but in the more traditional Renaissance meaning that focuses on the centrality of human experience as the source of authority for moral and ethical decision making. Gustavo Gutierrez describes this clearly:

> Humankind is seen as assuming conscious responsibility for its own destiny. This understanding provides a dynamic context and broadens the horizons of the desired social changes. In this perspective the unfolding of all the dimensions of humanness is demanded—persons who *make themselves* throughout their life and throughout history. [emphasis ours][35]

The process and concepts of liberation theology can significantly inform the process of identity and formation in Unitarian Universalist congregations. We can use the liberation theology process to open up our congregations to a variety of people who might otherwise find us puzzling or inaccessible.

The process and concepts of liberation theology can significantly inform the process of identity and formation in Unitarian Universalist congregations.

Implicit Covenants

As we begin to consider the possibility of welcoming into membership a more diverse population than we currently have, it is important to pay attention to some of the unstated but implicit covenants that govern our congregations.

At some level a statement of purpose contained in the bylaws, or even an affirmation read in services every Sunday, is nothing more than words on a page. More significant to the life of any community than the words it says it lives by are the affirmations (and negations) it actually lives by, expressed by its accustomed behaviors, customs, processes, and traditions. Implicit covenants are communicated almost subliminally, primarily by the real leaders—who may or may not be the nominal leaders—of the community. These folk are the gatekeepers, the matriarchs and patriarchs, the people who are continually teaching "how we do things here." This applies to all communities, not just congregations, but it certainly applies to congregations.

These implicit covenants are all the more powerful for the fact that they are largely invisible to those who are already established in the community. They are "just the way things are." Woe to a fledgling minister, or a would-be lay leader, who cannot see beneath the surface of the declared covenant of a congregation to its subliminal rules and assumptions.

Implicit covenants are a fact of life. A community would not really be a community without them. But they also represent the greatest barrier to change. To take an obvious example, many if not most of our congregations make stated commitments to diversity and openness, and some make even more explicit declarations of welcoming persons regardless of race, class, or sexual orientation. Yet by and large our congregations remain as they have been—white and middle-class. Some change has occurred with regard to sexual minorities, which is no doubt attributable in some measure to our relative uniqueness in ordaining significant numbers of openly gay and lesbian clergy, while many of the other even moderately liberal denominations have struggled with this issue.

We can learn at least two things from these facts. One is the power of implicit covenants, or to give it another name, the power of the status quo, which should never be underestimated. Communities change, as individuals change, with great difficulty. Like attracts like, so the way we were becomes the way we are and the way we often continue to be. The second thing, however, is that change is possible. To reiterate an important point made earlier in this report, each new member of a congregation changes it to some degree. Individuals do not simply become members of a community. By their joining and their participation the community is reconstituted, reformed, changed; it is no longer quite what it was before. In this fact there is hope.

There is also hope in the fact that there are some aspects of our history, our congregational culture, and our practices, that support and affirm the attempt to gather a diverse membership.

More than seventy years ago, Rev. Dr. Earl Morse Wilbur wrote an exhaustive history of the Unitarian side of our faith. He concluded that what makes our movement unique in history is our emphasis on freedom, reason, and tolerance: "When the Unitarian movement began, the marks of true religions were commonly thought to be belief in the creeds, membership in the church, and participation in its rites and sacraments. To the Unitarian of today [1925] the marks of true religion are spiritual freedom, enlightened reason, broad and tolerant sympathy, upright character, and unselfish service."[36]

Rev. John Buehrens has summarized our unique place in the contemporary American religious landscape:

> At a time when many of America's historic 'mainline' denominations are stagnant and divided, and when the politically motivated religious right seems the most prominent expression of religion in our culture, Unitarian Universalism offers a clear alternative—supporting the worth and dignity of every individual, respecting the rights of conscience, promoting the practice of authentic democracy, and recognizing our interdependence with all that exists. We do not have a required formula of belief. Instead, *we embody a reverent, respectful religious pluralism.* [emphasis ours][37]

One of the purposes of religion, any religion, is to offer people the opportunity to search for meaning, to make connections, and to seek spiritual transformation. Our particular contribution to that general purpose, always hoped for but not always realized, is that embodiment of reverent, respectful plural-

Communities change, as individuals change, with great difficulty.

ism. There is a great deal of talk these days about diversity and about how to create an atmosphere of respect for difference. We have always been a religion that advocates the use of reason and the primacy of human experience. We have been a faith that emphasizes process over content, covenant over creed. These are tools and traditions that our congregations can use in order to become places where diversity is welcomed and celebrated, places where every person's ideas and experiences are acknowledged, and where it is safe to bring personal experience into the religious conversation. A Unitarian Universalist theology of membership must take into account both the universal human religious need and the particular Unitarian Universalist response to that need.

Returning to Wilbur's history, we consider the idea of spiritual freedom as one of the most attractive aspects of our liberal faith. Ask a typical member of a Unitarian Universalist congregation what particularly attracted him/her to this way of faith and sooner rather than later he/she will say the word *freedom*. "Freedom of conscience." "Freedom of belief." What he/she would mean is the non-creedal principle, which is indeed central to our tradition. But a church is more than a club for freethinkers, or ought to be. You don't need a church to believe what you want, or to think for yourself. You need a church to be in relationship with others. As the word itself implies, a *community* is defined by something in common, gathered around some common purpose or belief.

You don't need a church to believe what you want, or to think for yourself. You need a church to be in relationship with others.

As the theologian Martin Buber puts it, "The real essence of community is to be found in the fact—manifest or otherwise—that it has a center. The real beginning of a community is when its members have a common relation to the center overriding all other relations: the circle is described by the radii, not by the points along its circumference."[38] This is a crucial insight. A community is defined by its center and by the various individuals' relationships to that center. Churches are commonly thought of as communities centered around a creed or doctrine. Ours our centered around a covenant.

Explicit Covenants

We often say that our congregations are covenantal communities. A *covenant* is a set of mutual commitments, promises, or agreements that form the bond of a community, its center. Following the practice established early on by our Puritan forebears, many of our congregations have explicit covenants, whether in traditional or contemporary form and language, which individuals "own" or "subscribe to" in the act of joining. These are sometimes called "bonds of union" or "bonds of fellowship." One of the most well-known of these is a variant of the so-called Ames Covenant. In the original formulation of its author, Rev. Charles G. Ames, the Ames Covenant read, "In the freedom of the Truth, and the spirit of Jesus Christ, we unite for the worship of God and the service of Man." Another example, which also exists in several variants, was composed by Rev. James Vila Blake: "Love is the spirit of this church, and service is its law. This is our great covenant: To dwell together in peace, To seek the truth in love, And to help one another."

One point in declaring that our congregations are covenantal communities is to emphasize that they are not creedal communities. We are united not by common beliefs but by common purposes and intentions. The essential difference is between the words "we believe" (a creed, a statement of common belief) and "we unite" (a covenant, a statement of common commitment).

Conrad Wright points out two "characteristic problems" with such statements. The first is a matter of language. As he says, "Some Unitarian Universalists are so allergic to particular styles of language that if they see a covenant that is not in accord with their preference, they stop reading." Some congregations expend considerable energy in attempting to reformulate their covenants to suit current tastes, though Wright himself suggests that since we welcome and encourage diversity, it might be "better to have such statements couched in language that represents nobody's preference, that belongs to no faction, so long as the substance behind the language is correct."[39] That is, as long as it is centered on the affirmation "we unite."

The second difficulty cited by Wright is of even more significance to the concerns of this report:

> The other problem with our covenants is that we do not take them seriously enough.... We need to pay more attention to what the commitments are that are undertaken in a covenant relationship and how they may be terminated. Joining a church should not be quite the same thing as joining the National Geographic Association [sic].[40]

If this problem is to be addressed at all, it needs to addressed in the process of joining rather than at the point of departure. A truly covenantal community will take its covenantal nature seriously and communicate its seriousness to those considering membership. But the reality in most of our congregations is that membership is treated at worst casually and even at best as largely a matter of solely individual choice. In our success-oriented culture both ministers and membership committees are often anxious to swell the ranks of the enlisted, so that visitors may find themselves being invited to join the congregation on their second or third appearance. It is encouraging in this regard to see growing numbers of congregations now suggesting a number of steps—such as taking a series of introductory classes or formal appointments with the minister—prior to membership.

The recently formed Epiphany Community Church in Fenton, Michigan, has taken another approach, one that has much to recommend it. This congregation has "translated" its covenant (the Ames Covenant) into a series of behavioral expectations, making explicit the commitments expected of both members and the congregation itself, one to another. "In the love of truth," for example, commits members to their own integrity: "I fearlessly seek the truth of my life. I reflect on my beliefs and actions and take responsibility for my spiritual growth." At the same time the congregation "commits to providing opportunities for truth-seeking. Worship classes, book studies and discussion groups are available." Each clause of the covenant is similarly fleshed out in this manner, such that the meaning of membership is vividly expressed. The entire text of the Epiphany model is attached as an appendix to this report.

The Membership Threshold

If we take our covenants seriously, treating them as blueprints for community rather than irrelevant but nice-sounding statements, then we will also begin to take more seriously the meaning of membership in our covenanted communities. While some UUs dearly value what they call the "easy in, easy out" culture, others recognize the need to imbue the membership experience with significance. Dean M. Kelley, points out in his book *Why Conservative Churches are Growing* that the fastest-growing churches tend to make joining the church difficult, not easy. These churches place a "high bar" at the membership threshold.

Written some thirty years ago, Kelley's book is still worth reading and subsequent research has largely confirmed his conclusions. The book has proved prophetic in predicting the long-term, ongoing decline in mainline religion and the rise of what he called "serious" or "strict" religious groups. His "Minimal Maxims of Seriousness" are worth reflecting upon. "Those who are serious about their faith," Kelley writes,

1. Do not confuse it with other beliefs/loyalties/practice, or mingle them together indiscriminately, or pretend they are alike, of equal merit, or mutually compatible if they are not.
2. Make high demands of those admitted to the organization that bears the faith, and do not include or allow to continue within it those who are not fully committed to it.
3. Do not consent to, encourage, or indulge any violations of its standards of belief or behavior by its professed adherents.
4. Do not keep silent about it, apologize for it, or let it be treated as though it made no difference, or should make no difference, in their behavior or in their relationships with others.[41]

This list is worth pondering. While some of their specific approaches would be inappropriate to liberal congregations, there is no question that conserva-

If we take our covenants seriously, we will also begin to take more seriously the meaning of membership in our covenanted communities.

tive churches communicate their seriousness about the meaning and commitments of membership. What does seem appropriate to liberal congregations is to take with greater seriousness the meaning and implications of their covenantal basis. We should, as Conrad Wright has suggested, take our covenants more seriously than we often do.

One way of doing so may be expressed in our rites and ceremonies of membership. The churches of many other denominations make a big deal of the act of joining as representing a moment of transformation in the life of the individual. Baptism, for example, at least in the traditions where it is central, symbolizes death and spiritual rebirth and enacts this process with a dramatic full immersion. Most of our congregations, by contrast, treat this event rather casually. In most, membership in the congregation is a voluntary individual decision, recognized ceremonially but with little fanfare. This is in keeping with our emphasis on individual conscience and free choice, but it fails to acknowledge the spiritual importance of membership—not only to the individual member but to the community itself.

Some of our older New England congregations, perhaps retaining forms from the past, require a formal declaration of intent to join the congregation, followed by a stipulated waiting period of weeks or even months before an individual's membership is confirmed. Presumably, the waiting period is to encourage serious contemplation of the decision and may include some spiritual discipline, required education, or pastoral conversation. If nothing else, such requirements signal that the congregation takes membership as something more serious than the casual signing of a book.

It is somewhat more common for the governing body of a congregation to formally receive new members. Though certainly *pro forma*, such practice does indicate and highlight the fact that membership is a reciprocal relationship, a mutual covenant between an individual and a congregation with at least implied obligations and responsibilities on both sides. Many congregations stipulate a waiting period between the time of signing the membership book and the conferring of voting rights.

A liturgical expression of the membership covenant is perhaps the most common of all reception practices, usually in the form of a ceremony of welcome incorporated into a Sunday worship service. Often these recognition events are rather informal. Taken with appropriate seriousness (as they commonly are by the new members themselves), they can serve as regular reminders and expressions of the fact that the congregation is a covenantal body, created by mutual promises and a sense of mutual obligation between and among its members, new and continuing.

The importance of allowing the children of the congregation to be in attendance on such occasions is often overlooked. Here is an opportunity for the children to witness a liturgical expression of the basic nature of the congregation, characterized by voluntary association and covenantal obligation. They may learn from such repeated experiences that congregation membership deserves to be and is taken seriously by the adult community. A similar case can be made for children's attendance at other important events in the congregation's liturgical life that define and express the community, such as christenings, dedications, and coming-of-age rituals.

To recapitulate: The distinguishing characteristic of our Unitarian congregations is that they are covenantal bodies. We are united as congregations not by common beliefs but by common commitments. Covenantal congregations are united not by statements of shared beliefs but instead by mutual promises. There are both implied and explicit commitments that the members of a congregation make to one another in joining themselves together; this is their covenant, made of mutual commitments of support, presence, and participation. The most familiar example of a covenantal relationship is marriage, in which the wedding vows are the covenant.

We moderns no longer take our covenants as seriously as did people in earlier times. As Conrad Wright has written with specific reference to our churches: "We do not remind ourselves that a covenant is an agreement made between parties, not a statement by an individual to be discarded and forgotten unilaterally. A church united by covenant is made up of people who have made commitments to one another."[42] He quotes the Cambridge Platform: "Church-members may not remove or depart from the Church, & so one from another as they please, nor without just & weighty cause but ought to live & dwell together."[43]

In those long-ago times people treated the bonds of church membership as seriously as they did the bonds of matrimony, which is to say very seriously indeed. The Commission invites Unitarian Universalists to return to the practice of taking membership seriously. We also invite Unitarian Universalists to consider a new, expanded, and generous definition of membership. This report is an urgent plea to create congregations that are inclusive and welcoming; most especially it is a plea to create non-traditional paths to membership that would usher in people who have previously felt unwelcome in our congregations. We believe that the survival, strength, and impact of our movement is dependent on strong, committed members at the local level.

If we were to re-create our congregations using the concepts of relational and liberation theology discussed earlier in this chapter, if we were to invite all of the people circling around the periphery of Unitarian Universalist congregations to tell their stories and to let their stories inform our decision making around membership practices, how would our congregations change? We are certain that we would see a small explosion of growth as people who long for affiliation with our religious communities found themselves welcomed. Our congregations would become more diverse—ethnically and theologically—as folks whose values are congruent with ours found new ways to express their spirituality within our walls. Music, dance, visual expressions, poetry,

We believe that the survival, strength, and impact of our movement is dependent on strong, committed members at the local level.

language—all would be transformed as our membership expanded. Infusions of energy from young people—both those who grew up in our congregations and those just finding our faith—would further transform our congregations in exciting ways.

One goal of this study of the meaning of membership is to enable our congregations to become more vital, more effective, and more diverse. Another goal is to help congregations create a membership process that allows individuals to deepen their experience of participation—to imbue the process of becoming a member with a spiritual meaning well beyond the technicalities of signing a book or voting. Unitarian Universalists want to belong to vital, growing, changing congregations that look outward as well as inward, congregations that support the spiritual growth and deepening faith of individual members and still ask questions about how they fit into the larger community. In order to achieve these goals, we propose an expanded definition of membership.

The Commission suggests that Unitarian Universalists begin to look at membership as an ongoing process of affiliation and connection between individuals (members) and the larger group (the congregation). The decision to become a part of the life of a Unitarian Universalist congregation is not necessarily made logically or in a linear mode. Amy Sales and Gary Tobin, in their survey of contemporary research about the way Americans affiliate with religious communities, emphasize the emotional, spiritual, and experiential aspects of the membership decision:

> . . . decisions about affiliation or dropping out are highly charged emotionally. Unlike decisions about which automobile to purchase or what color to paint one's house, decisions about church or synagogue membership touch on an individual's identity, ideology and beliefs, faith and spirituality, and on how all these will play out in the context of the family. These issues involve deep feeling.[44]

Honoring the spiritual milestone for each member would encourage people to become involved in the life of the local congregation.

The sense of belonging, of making a commitment on a spiritual level, may or may not be congruent in time with the act of signing a book or doing whatever is required to vote. David Bartholomew, writing about the issue of membership in contemporary American congregations, urges the separation of the voting role from the spiritual milestone.[45] Taking note of and honoring the spiritual milestone for each member, rather than celebrating only the technical act of book-signing, would encourage many different kinds of people to become involved in the life of the local congregation. Membership committees could then begin to focus on the relational aspects of the membership process rather than the technical problem of categorizing people based on whether or not they vote, pledge a certain amount, or have their signatures in a certain place.

Rather than focusing on defining qualifications for voting members, we suggest that congregations focus on appropriate participation as the variable that defines membership. Those that participate appropriately in the life of the congregation constitute its membership.

Appropriate participation can range from simple presence at worship, to making a contribution once a year, to bringing one's needs for ministry to the community. For example, a long-time member who is now confined to a nursing home participates appropriately by remaining on the mailing list and receiving visits from the minister and other caring members of the community. Another person may, due to limitations of health or circumstance, be present in the prayer life of the congregation, and this is appropriate participation also. Having needs and allowing oneself to be "ministered unto" is one way to participate appropriately in the life of the congregation.

Parents whose children are grown may choose not to attend but continue to write a check every year because they want to ensure the ongoing presence of the congregation in their town. We cannot define precisely appropriate participation or presence, but every congregation can broaden its understanding of membership to include many more people who wish to be part of the life of the congregation but don't fit into the traditional membership categories. Rather than trying to make rules about who is a member and who is not, one local congregation places people in a Caring Circle when they attend at least monthly. This is one measure of presence and invites further appropriate participation even from people who have not made the traditional "signing the book" commitment to membership. We encourage congregations to think creatively about what appropriate participation might be for individuals and families with differing circumstances who wish to be part of the congregation in some way.

Participation in the life of the community does assume some form of accountability to the community. Accountability has to do with a willingness to take some responsibility for the quality of life in the congregation. One new member interviewed soon after joining a UU congregation commented that although the decision to join had been completely subjective, he knew that the subjective experience demanded of him some pretty objective changes in behavior. He listed pledging at a higher rate, volunteering more seriously, and taking responsibility for the congregation. "Being a member is living it, not being passive." Recall the comment cited earlier regarding membership as a measure of how strongly a person wants to influence the destiny of the group.

Appropriate participation also assumes assent to the covenant of the congregation. Remember that in our discussion about the particular niche that Unitarian Universalism occupies in the American religious landscape, an emphasis on covenant rather than on creed was one of the identifiers. In order for members, especially new members, to assent to a covenant, the congregation has to have a covenant that is explicit. It is the responsibility of the group to define the ways it wishes to be together, to be clear with newcomers about the expectations of the group, and to remind each other frequently about the terms of the covenant. A caveat here: This does not mean that each new member who joins a congregation remakes himself/herself in the image of the covenant. In fact, if we understand the congregation to be an organic entity, every new person who participates actively in the life of the congregation changes the dynamic and, in effect, causes the covenant to be rewritten.

The Commission recommends that Unitarian Universalist congregations significantly expand their membership practices and definitions to embrace all people who wish to participate in a meaningful and healthy way in the life of the local congregation. The people who are participating appropriately are the constituency of your congregations. Rather than focusing on qualifications for voting, minimum pledge payments, age, theology, or any other attribute, we urge congregations to look at the range of people who share the worship life, the social life, and the justice-seeking life of the congregation. This is our membership, though all may not have signatures in the membership book. We recognize that this is a radical departure from the practices of many, if not most, membership committees. We also recognize that this practice raises some complicated issues around identity, accountability, inclusion, and definition.

Notes

1. "For just as the body is one and has many members, and all the members of the body, though many, are one body, so it is with Christ."
2. Unitarian Universalist Association, *Fulfilling the Promise: A Recovenanting Process for the 21st Century* (Boston: Unitarian Universalist Association, 1998).
3. Bernard Jones, *Belonging: A Lay Theology of Church Membership* (London: Epworth Press, 1973), 74.
4. "Now there are varieties of gifts, but the same Spirit; and there are varieties of services, but the same Lord; and there are varieties of activities, but it is the same God who activates all of them in everyone." I Cor. 12: 4-6.
5. John Throop, "Believing In Lay Ministry," *The Christian Ministry* (November-December, 1997): 16.
6. Jones, op. cit., 22.
7. George Rupp, *Commitment and Community*. (Minneapolis, MN: Fortress Press, 1989), 78.
8. Loren B. Mead, *More Than Numbers. The Way Churches Grow* (Washington, DC: Alban Institute), 42.
9. Linda Olson-Peebles, Church Newsletter (Alexandria, VA: Mt. Vernon Unitarian Church).
10. John Burkhardt, *Worship: A Searching Examination of the Liturgical Experience* (Philadelphia: Westminster Press, 1982), 23.
11. Rupp, op. cit., 50.

12. "The living tradition we share draws from many sources: direct experience of that transcending mystery and wonder, affirmed in all cultures, which moves us to a renewal of the spirit and an openness to the forces that create and uphold life."

13. Henry Nelson Wieman, as quoted in Bruce Southworth, *At Home in Creativity: The Naturalistic Theology of Henry Nelson Wieman* (Boston: Skinner House Books), 30.

14. Rupp, op. cit., 5.

15. Harold Rosen, *Religious Education and Our Ultimate Commitment. An Application of Henry Nelson Wieman's Philosophy of Creative Interchange.* (Lanham, MD: University Press of America, 1985), 11.

16. James Luther Adams, as quoted in Ibid., 39.

17. Ibid., 33.

18. Henry Nelson Wieman as quoted in ibid., 46.

19. Rosen, op. cit., 46.

20. Ibid., 42.

21. Wieman, as quoted in ibid., 43.

22. Mary Hunt, *Fierce Tenderness: A Feminist Theology of Friendship* (New York: Crossroad Publishing, 1992), 99.

23. Ibid., 104.

24. James Cone as quoted in Diana Hayes, *And Still We Rise: An Introduction to Black Liberation Theology* (New York: Paulist Press, 1996), 5.

25. Richard Gilbert, *Building Your Own Theology*, 2nd ed. (Boston: Unitarian Universalist Association, 2000), 3.

26. Thandeka, as quoted in Frederic John Muir, *A Reason For Hope: Liberation Theology Confronts a Liberal Faith* (Carmel, CA: Sunflower Ink, 1994), 61.

27. Ada Maria Isasi-Diaz, *En La Lucha* (*In the Struggle: Elaborating a Mujerista Theology*) (Minneapolis, MN: Fortress Press, 1993), 5. Mujerista theology refers to theological work done by women of Hispanic heritage.

28. Gustavo Gutierrez, *A Theology of Liberation History: Politics and Salvation*, Rev. Ed (New York: Orbis Books, 1988), 121.

29. Gutierrez, op. cit., 57.

30. Ibid., 10.

31. Richard S. Gilbert, *How Much Do We Deserve? An Inquiry into Distributive Justice*, 2nd. ed. (Boston: Unitarian Universalist Association, 2001), 11.

32. Isasi-Diaz, op. cit., 167.

33. Ibid., 156.

34. William R. Jones, *Is God a White Racist? A Preamble to Black Theology* (Boston: Beacon Press, 1998), 187.

35. Gutierrez, op. cit., 24.

36. Earl Morse Wilbur, *Our Unitarian Heritage* (Boston: Beacon Press, 1925), 470.

37. John A. Buehrens, ed., *The Unitarian Universalist Pocket Guide*, 3rd ed. (Boston: Skinner House Books, 1999), x.

38. Martin Buber as quoted in Jacob Trapp, ed., *To Hallow this Life* (New York: Harper, 1958), 135.

39. Conrad Wright, *Walking Together*. (Boston: Skinner House Books, 1989), 9.

40. Ibid., 9.

41. Dean M. Kelley, *Why Conservative Churches are Growing* (New York: Harper & Row, 1972), 121.

42. Wright, op. cit., 9.

43. Cambridge Platform, as quoted in ibid. The Cambridge Platform is a document written in 1648 that established the polity of the New England Puritans. It is the normative basis for congregational polity.

44. Amy Sales and Gary Tobin, eds., *Church and Synagogue Affiliation: Theory, Research, and Practice* (Westport, CT: Greenwood Press, 1995), 7.

45. David Bartholomew, "Membership Matters," *Epworth Review*, 20, no. 2 (April 1997): 60.

Measures of Membership

The work of the Alban Institute's Loren Mead has helped to establish a framework for considering membership questions in this report. Mead builds on the work of Ted Buckle in suggesting that there are four distinct dynamics to church growth: numerical growth, maturational growth, organic growth, and incarnational growth.

Although a definition of *numerical growth* might be obvious, it is somewhat problematic. Congregation rolls are notoriously unreliable. The Alban Institute suggests that attendance at worship and Sunday school, pledges collected, and involvement and presence are far better measures of membership than numbers of members. Even at the level of simple counting and accounting, issues of commitment and participation come into play. Whatever numbers are used to measure numerical growth, the conclusion is inevitable. In Mead's words, "Any human institution that does not develop an effective method of recruiting new membership (and leadership) will die. There are no exceptions."[1] Numerical growth is the way a healthy institution maintains itself so that it can continue to act out its mission in the world.

Maturational growth refers to the experience of individuals as they are transformed by membership. Mead suggests an increase in maturity of faith, a deepening spirituality, and an expansion of the religious imagination as the markers of maturational growth. He defines religious imagination as that which allows a person to see life as a complex array of choices, rather than a simple yes-or-no question.

The third type of growth is *organic growth*. Mead draws on systems theory in order to understand the congregation as a living system whose structures must constantly change and adapt to the inputs (new members, more mature members) in order to sustain growth. Mead describes it as the intentional creation of community, an essential goal of congregational leadership: "Organic growth is about the task of building the community, fashioning the organizational structures, developing the processes and practices that result in a dependable, stable network of human relationships in which we can grow and from which we can make a difference."[2] Struggling with how to achieve organic growth raises several thorny issues that the Commission believes congregations will have to struggle with. We don't advocate particular "one size fits all" answers to these questions. Our goal is to raise the issues and provide background on how congregational leadership might frame their own particular answers.

The final form of growth is *incarnational growth*. This is about going out into the community and "enfleshing" its values. Incarnational growth addresses the relationship between a particular congregation and its environment. It is grounded in the other forms of growth—it cannot occur over a sustained period of time without the supportive internal structures and the mature and committed participation of a critical mass of members. Simply stated, incarnational growth is about how we live out our faith in the world.

In the context of Mead's model, growth is understood to be a complex and multifaceted phenomenon that is inseparable from the meaning of membership.

Quantity of Membership

That numbers count is a reality of contemporary Unitarian Universalism. It is impossible to discuss membership without addressing ways in which numbers are used: to measure growth and decline, both in the UUA and in individual congregations; to measure trends in various areas of the continent; to determine levels and types of services from the UUA; to establish Fair Share payments to districts and the UUA; to provide congregational statistics for reporting in the UUA and district directories and to outside publications. In addition, membership numbers are shared, contrasted, and compared by ministerial colleagues when discussing the vitality of their congregations, and they are a major descriptive feature of congregations, used, for example, in the ministerial search process when a congregation describes itself to potential ministers, both settled and interim.

The fact that various congregations count their constituencies in different ways complicates the issue of membership numbers and what they might mean. An informal Commission survey of membership in randomly selected congregations during 2000 revealed numerous ways to categorize members as well as friends. There are voting members, honorary voting members, active members, out-of-town members, lifetime members, emerita/us members, inactive members, youth members, and student members, and this probably does not exhaust the list. Friends (usually people who participate in the life of the congregation but have chosen not to sign the membership book) are variously called pledging friends, contributing friends, newsletter friends, and RE friends. A further complication is that some congregations refer to pledging units while others count the full constituency (members, friends, those receiving the newsletter, plus children in the RE program), families affiliated with the congregation, attendance at worship, and the parish. Within our system of congregational polity there is a remarkable variety of ways to count membership or participation in congregations.

Current policy of the UUA uses number of members to determine a congregation's Fair Share assessment in support of both the Association and districts. One result of this practice is "updating" of membership lists, sometimes called weeding. There is a monetary incentive for keeping congregational membership numbers as low as possible when reporting to the UUA. The membership number used in conversations can be twice the number reported. This raises serious ethical as well as financial concerns.

There is a monetary incentive for keeping congregational membership numbers as low as possible when reporting to the UUA.

One such concern relates to people who are unable to pay the pledges commonly expected as a condition of membership. Many congregations have established special categories for such people, who may be elderly, disabled, or in a financial crisis. The category may be assigned as a special tribute for long or exceptional membership participation over time; it may involve asking a minister or congregation official to waive any financial requirement. Individuals in the latter category may be embarrassed to ask for special consideration and choose to resign rather than be perceived as not self-supporting. Unitarian Universalists have a reputation for being fiercely independent in their theology and their social views, and this sense of independence can be expected to manifest itself in attitudes about paying one's own way. People who choose formal resignation or quiet disappearance may be deprived of community, needed services, pastoral care, and/or spiritual growth. It is entirely possible that there's a quiet feeling of coercion in the decision to resign or leave, even if none is intended. To what extent should membership depend on the ability to pay for it?

It would be naïve to suggest that a congregation can exist without dependable income. Nonetheless, if we seriously intend to be economically diverse, there must be ways to readjust the relationship between membership and money.

Two significant questions raised here are

- What are the fairest and most responsible ways to balance the ideal of the congregation as a caring and compassionate community with congregation as a viable economic entity?

- By what formula should congregations support the UUA and its districts so that there is no perceived advantage in keeping membership numbers low?

In his report to the General Assembly in 2000, UUA financial advisor Lawrence (Larry) Ladd writes, "Our community of faith continues to grow. We are growing in numbers, in generosity, and in congregational resources."[3] Using 1985 as a reference point for comparison, Ladd presents these figures for 2000:

- Membership: 154,459, up 10.9 percent
- Religious education enrollment: 61,165, up 56.8 percent
- Combined adult membership and RE enrollment: 215,624, up 21 percent

He observes that growth in RE enrollments generally exceeds the growth in membership.[4] Subsequently, using figures from the consolidation of the American Unitarian Association (AUA) and the Universalist Church in America (UCA) in 1961, Ladd reports, "We grew substantially in the Sixties, declined in the Seventies, and have been making slow, steady progress since 1982."[5]

Several times Ladd cautions that some data is suspect, and for several reasons. One of those reasons is the variety of ways in which congregations count their members. But as he also comments, the data "is the best we have."[6] One observation from the data with which he seems comfortable is that the number of congregations has remained fairly constant since 1961—around one thousand. Some congregations have been born; some have died.

One additional graph in the financial advisor's report shows combined UUA membership and RE enrollment as a percentage of the U.S. population. The report apparently does not include Canada in the total population but may include Canadian Unitarian Universalists in the UUA number. This data shows the highest percentage (0.14 percent) between 1967 and 1970, and a fairly constant 0.08 percent between 1980 and 1997, the most recent year included in the graph. A possible interpretation of this data is that growth in numbers (adult and RE) has resulted in "holding our own" relative to general U.S. population growth. Ladd contends, "We should be proud of our growth. We should be dissatisfied with the modesty of that growth given our potential."[7]

It might be interesting to compare our numbers with those of various other faith communities over a given period of time, or to compare the average age of members, were this data available. Numbers have many uses in assessment and planning, but inconsistency in both counting and interpretation makes their significance uncertain.

Robert D. Putnam writes in *Bowling Alone*, "Denominational membership figures are debatable because denominations vary in the strictness of their definition of membership, membership figures are only irregularly updated, self-reports may be inflated, and not all churches keep or report accurate records. Poll data avoid some of these drawbacks but generally record higher membership figures than the ecclesiastical records, probably because many lapsed members continue to identify themselves as Presbyterian, or Jewish, or Catholic."[8] This observation meshes with often-cited poll data showing that many more people self-identify as Unitarian Universalists than can be accounted for in any UUA data.

To what extent and in what way does counting individual members of a congregation (or of the UUA) affect the identification of people with and participation in Unitarian Universalism? Looking at numbers alone focuses narrowly on only one category: legal membership, those who have formally signed the book and met any other requirements for membership in a given congregation. But we know that every congregation includes significant numbers of people who are affiliated, involved, supportive in many ways, but not legal members. Our theology of membership and inclusion requires that we concern ourselves with this broader constituency. The *quality* of membership is not necessarily reflected in numbers alone.

The quality of membership is not necessarily reflected in numbers alone.

Membership is about deepening individuals' connections with their congregations as well as encouraging their own spiritual journeys. It is about developing an understanding and theology of membership that renews individuals and our movement. To these ends, healthy membership theologies and practices must also concern themselves with what Loren Mead calls maturational, organic, and incarnational growth.

Quality of Membership

People value memberships for both their intrinsic and their extrinsic worth. When the membership is in a religious community, however, the intrinsic, deep, and emotional components are, at their best, of greater significance than any others. They help members deal with the peaks and valleys of human experience. Consider the following comments offered in UU churches during the Joys and Sorrows portion of the service:

> I thank everyone who offered me support last spring when I told you I'd be starting treatment for breast cancer. Things went well for quite some time, but I saw my doctor this past week, and it's not so good. I need your love and encouragement again.

> I found it very powerful to share my joy about C_____ in church (Unitarian Universalist) and receive so much responds [sic]. It was positively overwhelming to experience such a strong and supporting community.

Comments such as these, publicly expressed, reflect the high quality of congregation membership/friend status experienced by the speakers. They have found in their congregational connections what people hope to receive from religiously based organizations: support, acknowledgment, affirmation, caring, response. Ideally, these qualities are an outgrowth of the theological underpinnings of that religious expression. Similar responses can be found in any group whose members care about one another, but there is a special quality within the religious community that crosses lines of race, ethnicity, politics, social status, sexual orientation, or any other demographic that brings people together in communities or organizations for varying periods of time.

What happens to the quality of congregation membership when conflicts arise, as they invariably do whenever human beings are together over time? The sources of these conflicts are common, familiar, all too frequent, and by no means limited to Unitarian Universalists: Should we buy the building next door to expand the church school? Sell the parsonage? Fire the minister? Use mugs or styrofoam cups at coffee hour? Become a Welcoming Congregation? Redesign readings to use inclusive language? Use weed killer on the lawn? Spend extra money on ourselves or on others?

Internal conflicts, often called church politics, are frequently cited as the reason people cut their pledges or resign their memberships in a particular congregation. Are they experiencing what is called elsewhere in this report first disillusionment? Are they astonished that people in *this* congregation could disagree with them on matters either significant or trivial? How is disagreement handled? Are Unitarian Universalists more prone than other religious organizations to experience conflict or to have drastic results when members hold different points of view?

There have been a number of studies of conflict in religious organizations. Wade Clark Roof, in his 1978 book *Community and Commitment*, wrote that liberal congregations may be more conflict-prone because they are more democratic.[9] In 1993 Penny Edgell Becker et al. found at least some conflicts resulting from a division between older and newer members.[10]

Over a period of 18 months in the early 1990s Becker interviewed 231 people from 23 congregations: 203 lay members and 28 clergy. In addition, she attended worship services and meetings and reviewed printed documents such as annual reports, mission statements, constitutions, written histories, promotional brochures, and sermons. This is how she describes a community she calls Pleasantdale, the location of the study: population about 50,000, 18 percent black, 77 percent white; largely a community of young professionals in professional families; known in academic and policy circles for "achieving stable racial integration in the early 1970s";[11] known for being progressive. She collected data in 2 synagogues, 2 Catholic parishes, and 19 Protestant congregations in Pleasantdale and 2 adjacent, smaller communities. One of the congregations was Unitarian Universalist, described as large (more than 150 regular Sunday/Sabbath attenders, with administration divided into boards and committees). Among her findings were the following:

> Liberal congregations were the only ones to fight about inclusive language and becoming "open and affirming," while conservative congregations had the only conflicts over premarital or extramarital sex. There were no other differences in what liberal and conservative churches fought over.

> More of the serious conflicts, with members leaving and resolution elusive, were in liberal congregations. The size and polity of a congregation did not influence the kinds of issues bringing conflict.

> Regarding the amount of conflict: There were twenty-nine conflicts in small congregations, thirty-six in large ones, thirty-one in liberal, and thirty-four in conservative.[12]

Congregational Models

Becker worked with four organizational models in her study: congregation as *family*, as *community*, as *leader*, and as *house of worship*. All four models agree that worship and religious education are the core tasks of a congregation; these are the only core tasks specified in her house-of-worship model. The family model means the whole congregation is close, family-like. The congregation-as-community model agrees with the family model but adds, "Adopt policies that express members' values and interpretations on social issues" and substitutes "closeness and familylike within small groups" for having the whole congregation be family-like.[13] Congregations operating on the leader model do not consider closeness as a core task. Rather, they emphasize adopting official policies or pastor's guidelines on social issues and being a leader in the community and beyond.

Not surprisingly, Becker found four of the congregations were "mixed": a Missouri Synod Lutheran, a Catholic, an Episcopalian, and the Unitarian Universalist. When conflict developed in these congregations, the results were intense:

> Mixed congregations are the only ones where conflict raged through a series of events, and where resolution was virtually impossible without the exit of one of the groups that had been mobilized. Formal rules were invoked and votes taken, but to little avail, as the conflict erupted again. The governance structure of the congregation was questioned openly in three of these congregations, and in one was under a process of review and revision during the conflict.[14]

The specific conflict Becker identified in the UU congregation was between a group preferring a family model and a newer group preferring a leader model.

Later, Becker comments, "Members can identify the bundle of things that matter to them about their local congregation, and they orient their behavior to these locally institutionalized ideas about 'who we are.' When challenged, members can clearly articulate their preference for a certain style of congregation, and they are very conscious that a victory for the other side means their congregation will turn into a place that is in many ways less representative of their values.'[15]

Managing Change

Change is never easy, and it's often disruptive. Whenever new people become part of an established congregation, they understandably bring with them their values and perceptions. If they have been told they will be accepted as they are, what do they understand this to mean? If they are more conservative, or more liberal, than the current culture of the congregation, how can they express their differences? Can they rightly expect that the culture will change to reflect their views to a greater degree? How do longer-time members respond? Are *they* right in thinking the new people want to change the very institution and values that attracted them in the first place? When significant change occurs, what is an appropriate response to the person who says sadly, "This isn't the congregation I joined. I no longer feel comfortable here"? Becker found this as a conflict flash point in her study.

Can it be generalized from Becker's work and from the Commission questionnaire that, for whatever reasons, UUs find it especially difficult to manage conflict? Does Unitarian Universalism in its contemporary form attract people of deeply held views who find sharing or compromise difficult if not impossible? When their views are challenged, do they feel under attack as individuals? Are they in fact under attack? Are Unitarian Universalists in general truly "liberal," using the definition "generous of spirit"? These are significant issues affecting an individual's deepest feelings of belonging, of being a member of a religious community.

Another question: To what extent are these divisive issues of a religious nature, to what degree are they social/societal, and how much are they mixed? In recent years there has been considerable activity in the UU world regarding diversity. To the extent that this diversity reflects differences of race, ethnicity, social class, sexual orientation, or other societal differences, there appears to be an improving comfort level, although much work remains. However, to the extent that differences are in *religious practice*, incorporating religious expressions outside conventional Western religious tradition for example, or at variance with the culture of a given congregation at a particular time, these differences can be viewed as divergent, as proceeding in different directions religiously. In congregations with Buddhist or pagan or similar groups, to the extent the participants are also part of the ongoing life of the congregation, they are generally accepted. To the extent participants are not otherwise involved in the life of the congregation, the group is sometimes viewed as taking advantage of a free meeting space and questions arise as to whether this is appropriate. The issue came up in private conversations with respondents to the Commission questionnaire and with members of responding congregations but comments were not committed to paper. These issues, too, affect perceptions of the *quality* of membership.

A further question: Is it possible that, within the UU world, promises are made that cannot be fulfilled? When a newcomer hears, "You are accepted as you are," what does that mean? Who accepts? What are the limits of what is acceptable? What is required of the person seeking acceptance? *People* make promises; *people* fulfill them. Institutions can do neither. If promises are made or implied that require others to *do* something, to what extent is an obligation also implied? How an individual reacts to such an implication of obligation is another aspect of the quality of membership. Is this within the free church tradition and operational mode of congregational polity in which Unitarian Universalism has its roots?

UUA financial advisor Larry Ladd, in his verbal report to the UUA General Assembly in 2000, spoke of the importance of a "clear religious message" to congregation growth.[16] What *is* a clear religious message? What is the clear *religious* message of contemporary Unitarian Universalism? Who expresses it? How is it heard and interpreted? How and when can these questions be answered, and by whom?

No matter its size, a congregation whose members treat one another with gentleness and respect and that has a good idea of how it fits into its time and place as well as its future, will provide the quality of membership that reduces the revolving-door syndrome, makes people want to join, and affirms the best that Unitarian Universalism represents.

Notes

1. Loren B. Mead, *More Than Numbers: The Way Churches Grow* (Washington, DC: Alban Institute, 1993), 16.
2. Ibid., 60.
3. Lawrence Ladd, Financial Advisor's Report to the UUA General Assembly, Nashville, TN, June 2000, 3.
4. Ibid., 4.
5. Ibid., 5.
6. Ibid., 6.

7. Ibid., 7.
8. Robert D. Putnam, *Bowling Alone* (New York: Simon & Schuster, 2000), 69.
9. Wade Clark Roof, *Community and Commitment* (New York: Elsevier, 1978).
10. Penny Egell Becker et al., "Congregational Models and Conflict: A Study of How Institutions Shape Organizational Process" in N. J. Demerath, III, et al., eds., *Sacred Companies: Organizational Aspects of Religion and Religious Aspects of Organizations* (New York: Oxford University Press, 1998), 231–55.
11. Ibid., 234.
12. Ibid., 235.
13. Ibid., 237.
14. Ibid., 245.
15. Ibid., 246.
16. Ladd, op. cit., 15.

Creating Thriving Congregations

If we are going to experience the quality of congregational life that we aspire to, it will not happen by chance. We must pay attention to the structures and processes, what Mead calls *organic growth*: "Organic growth is about the task of building the community, fashioning the organizational structures, developing the practices and processes that result in a dependable, stable network of human relationships in which we can grow and from which we can make a difference."[1]

Systems theory helps congregations with the task of building community and is therefore useful in deepening our understanding of the meaning of membership.

Social systems...are complex organisms with distinct parts and orderly processes that somehow form a single entity out of that complexity, within a particular environment....Systems have a boundary that distinguishes and separates them from their environment. They receive input from the environment, they act on those inputs in their own characteristic ways, and they send their outputs back into the environment....In this sense, a congregation is a social system.[2]

The strength and vitality of each and every UU congregation are central to the strength and vitality of the movement. This is why membership is of such interest to the Commission. In applying systems theory to questions of membership, we are interested in how those congregations relate to the individual's identity as a Unitarian Universalist. Participation in worship and involvement in the expressions of the congregation's ministry are significant processes that affect commitment and the extent to which individuals engage in the life of the congregation.

This discussion focuses on two functions of the social system that relate to membership formation:

- the definitions congregations use to distinguish themselves from the environment around them, known as boundaries
- the ways in which congregations engage people more deeply in the life of the congregation

What We Are and What We Are Not

Too often a discussion about Unitarian Universalism encounters confusion about what makes a Unitarian Universalist. Lack of knowledge about our movement leads to misunderstandings about who we are (and who we are not!). Jokes abound. Tolerance gets confused with an absence of limits on personal behavior. Children get feel-good education that leaves them without skills and resources to wrestle with the difficult questions of life, and our congregations get bogged down in politeness and political correctness. The Commission believes that congregations can address this confusion and help Unitarian Universalists find deeper meaning in the life of the congregation; an understanding of systems theory helps in this process.

Boundaries help us define who we are, as individuals and as congregations. Definition of membership is an important function of boundary definition. In the free church, the individual determines whether she/he meets the membership criteria defined by the congregation. There is no faith "test." Commitment to the congregation, however, can be sustained better over time if individual members feel a strong connection to the congregation. The inevitable differences of opinion that arise in any human community can be transcended, forgiven, or resolved and in the end contribute to a stronger, healthier congregation. Thus we believe it is important to look at membership practices that help to deepen commitment to the congregation.

Boundary maintenance is a process of managing the tension between what might seem to be competing principles. Being open and accepting can lead to such diffuse boundaries that the congregation has no sense of "center." Defining membership in more specific terms, however, can result in exclusion and narrowness of perspective. How do we find that balance? One UU stated, "A fear

Definition of membership is an important function of boundary definition.

of mine is that if we don't have some kind of framework as to what constitutes a UU society or person, then how can we call ourselves anything?...Have we become so liberal finally that we aren't really anything? Are we in danger of 'tolerating' ourselves out of existence as a significant religious movement which offers, all in all, an alternative to mainline religions?" By developing structures and processes for membership, a congregation can better define its boundaries and provide an environment where individuals can pursue their own religious development.

Engaging in Congregational Life

There are two key factors in how a congregation defines its boundaries and engages people in the congregation that have particular relevance to our understanding of the organic dimensions of membership: norms/expectations and beliefs/values. These factors shape the ministries of the congregation and help the congregation to define itself and articulate its meaning of membership.

Norms and expectations are the guidelines for what is acceptable and what is not acceptable in the congregation. "In all sound systems," says Mead, "the boundary between what is acceptable and what is unacceptable is enforced by everyone and by no one."[3] It is typical for norms to be unspoken, often communicated by non-verbal behaviors. One often does not know about a norm until he/she has violated it. These unwritten rules can be confusing to newcomers and often become an impediment to creating healthy, open communities. A norm that "we are like a family" can create small, close-knit groups that make it extremely difficult for a newcomer to make a connection within the congregation. Such descriptions should, in fact, raise questions about whether the boundaries are too rigid and exclusive. The Commission has found, in our conversations around the continent, that many congregations have norms, or implicit covenants, for group membership that are not articulated and may be undermining stated goals for growth. It is not uncommon to hear stories of visitors to our congregations feeling ignored during the coffee hour, despite statements of welcome from the pulpit. We have heard often of people who come to our congregations searching for religious community who end up feeling discouraged and excluded. This may be due to inexplicit norms or rigid boundaries in the congregational system.

Many congregations have clarified the norms of the congregation by articulating the responsibilities of membership, developing an explicit covenant. These congregations are becoming more intentional about the meaning of membership. Membership covenants vary, reflecting the diversity of language and image that characterizes congregational life. These articulated expecta-

Unwritten rules can be confusing to newcomers and often become an impediment to creating healthy, open communities.

tions are examples of "high" membership requirements. They usually take the form of a statement of responsibilities of congregation membership, and many include the following expectations:

- Worship with the congregation.
- Pursue your own spiritual growth.
- Join in the work of the congregation.
- Pledge at a level commensurate with commitment to the congregation.
- Perform service to the wider community.
- Connect with the larger UU movement.

Beliefs and values are another element of a social system. They are its "center of gravity." Most faith communities build their social systems around a clearly defined belief system. A central premise of Unitarian Universalism has historically been our "free faith." No creed or dogma will exclude members, and members will not be required to subscribe to any creed. Our commitment to a free and responsible search for truth and meaning can make it difficult to find that center of gravity that can help a congregation develop cohesiveness and a sense of purpose. Rev. Barbara Wells writes, "At times we have taken our freedom to mean lack of commitment. Too often churches have been unclear what commitment to membership means and have been unable to give fellow journeyers maps to lead them into a deeper relationship with the church."[4]

When the congregation does not create an environment in which beliefs and values are openly expressed and examined on an ongoing basis, behavior may not correspond to the stated norms. It is not uncommon to hear UUs relate stories of the elation they felt upon first finding a liberal religious environment in which they could express their deepest spiritual searching, only to experience profound disappointment that their "truth" is somehow not accepted by others in the congregation despite the statements of openness and tolerance. The Commission has heard from many who experience disapproval or non-acceptance when their religious or spiritual paths lead them away from the prevailing norms of their congregations.

This change in the nature of individual religious experience over time is not surprising; in fact it is encouraged and expected in a free faith where the unveiling of truth is seen as a work in progress. Our faith calls us to live in the creative tension between what we have understood and what we are coming to understand. The living tradition of our Unitarian Universalist faith does not see religious truth as a static condition but rather as one of continuous revelation. The religious views and values that lead one into membership of a UU congregation at one stage in life should evolve over time. That one's beliefs and values would be questioned, examined, and even changed as part of the spiritual growth process is desirable. Looking at this from a perspective of organic growth, congregations need to develop approaches to membership that respect

Our faith calls us to live in the creative tension between what we have understood and what we are coming to understand.

and celebrate ongoing faith development so that people can deepen in their commitment rather than feel excluded or unwelcome.

Systems theory tells us that a healthy organization lives with this tension, sees it as a creative force, and develops procedures and practices that encourage clarity and openness simultaneously.

Moving toward Deeper Commitment

How can congregations best adopt organic structures that promote a broader understanding of the meaning of membership? Church membership literature discusses two dimensions of membership that affect depth of commitment: entry and maintenance. *Entry* refers to the requirements for entry into membership in the faith community and *maintenance* refers to the visible forms of commitment necessary to keep that membership status.

Each of these dimensions is seen as being low or high. Many of the new, rapidly growing non-denominational churches have high entry requirements and high maintenance requirements. Although many people attend the services and share in the religious life of the community, actual admission into membership takes place only after demonstration of willingness to meet high demands of membership (both in financial, personal, and faith dimensions). Unitarian Universalist congregations, perhaps in response to rigid creed and restrictive theologies of previous religious experience, often have low entry and low maintenance requirements. Most UU churches require only the signing of a membership book and perhaps some minimal evidence of financial support. The Commission heard many stories of casual approaches to signing the membership book. The Commission believes there is a place between casual and conforming and that place can be better defined if our congregations pay attention to the structures and processes of membership.

There is a place between casual and conforming.

What initially attracts a person to a UU congregation is unlikely to be what keeps that person as a committed, growing participant in the life of the congregation over time. UU ministers working in the extension program to strengthen and grow existing congregations as well as to launch new congregations provide valuable insights in this discussion. These approaches, often referred to as the path to membership, reflect the progressive nature of identification with Unitarian Universalism as a movement. Healthy congregations understand this developmental process and create programs (or ministries) that respond to peoples' needs over time. Many congregations have developed orientation programs for people in the initial stages of identification with a Unitarian Universalist congregation. Growing numbers of our congregations invite people into small groups, often referred to as covenant groups, where they can build relationships with others. As people deepen their commitment, perhaps moving into formal membership, they are encouraged to explore the history of the Unitarians and the Universalists through religious education classes and branch out into the life of the congregation through service in various programs. Formal membership may not take place until people have been participating in the community for some time and understand the significance of the congregation and the movement in their personal and spiritual lives. Some congregations have requirements for formal membership such as participation in an orientation session or a meeting with the minister; most, however, encourage but do not require such actions. Methodist evangelist John Wesley recognized the different steps in the path to becoming a committed believer. Each step is important in its own right and must be recognized for the different needs and readiness it represents. The path to membership would be a Unitarian Universalist version of the stages identified by Wesley. Regardless of the specific process, increasingly our congregations are implementing strategies that support people as they move along this path. Many congregations, however, still look at membership as an either/or proposition. You are either a member or you're not. It is the Commission's fervent hope that these congregations will be moved to a new understanding of membership and implement recommendations from this report.

Membership Issues

We encourage dialogue within congregations and throughout the movement, thus increasing awareness and more intentional practices regarding membership.

Keeping in mind that a systems perspective on membership focuses on those procedures that a congregation puts in place to define its boundaries and thus its identity, the Commission has found a number of issues that trigger discussion and, at times, confuse our understanding of the meaning of membership. These issues lead to provocative questions that can provide the basis for discussion and discernment. We do not propose answers to these questions; rather we encourage dialogue within congregations and throughout the movement, thus increasing awareness and more intentional practices regarding membership. The particular definitions of membership matter less to us than do the steps taken by our congregations to define and clarify expectations on the part of each congregation. Thus, expectations are made more explicit and open to congregational awareness.

The Issue: Annual Program Fund

Numerical growth is the dimension most often discussed in regard to the relationship between the Annual Program Fund (APF) and the meaning of membership. Discussion and debate abound about how many UUs there are in North America. Many maintain that there would be more (numerically) if the APF used a different way of assessing a congregation's contribution to the UUA (referred to as the Fair Share). Some maintain that the reason the denomination's growth curve (as measured by number of adult members) is not an accurate reflection of membership size is because congregations are manipulating numbers in order to reduce the Fair Share assessment. Those most familiar with the history of these efforts have told us that, whatever indicator is used to calculate the Fair Share (average attendance, annual budget, and so forth), the growth curve measured by that variable levels out while other indicators change.

The UUA established a per member recommended contribution for congregations. This sum, often referred to in Commission hearings as a "head tax," is perceived by many to be the culprit behind the confusing numbers associated with the question, "How many Unitarian Universalists are there?" At every hearing held by the Commission during this study, someone would raise this issue as being at the heart of the "membership problem." Many congregations establish a "minimum contribution" for voting membership that corresponds to the congregation's assessed Fair Share. They want to make sure, it seems, that it does not cost the congregation to have someone's name on the membership roles. Many have proposed to the Commission that the question of membership would be less troublesome if the UUA did not assess this "head tax." Several years ago, large congregations were offered an alternative method for assessing their Fair Share contribution. Many recommended to the Commission that this strategy be adopted for all congregations. There may be merit to these suggestions, but the Commission believes that, in terms of membership, it misses the point. One UU in communication with the Commission raised the concern "that if we try to devise a formula that is going to be—without exception—totally and completely 'fair' for every single congregation at any particular stage of its life, we'll end up with formulae as complicated...as the IRS's Form 1040." The real issue, we believe, is building a strong, vital voice for our liberal religious values. The APF is one strategy for generating the financial commitment needed to assist in this effort.

The real issue is building a strong, vital voice for our liberal religious values.

Focusing on minimal contributions sufficient to cover the per member contribution used in the calculation for association and district contributions distracts us from the real work before us. In a conversation with the Commission on Appraisal, Rev. John Buehrens calls this kind of attention to detail, "policing the fringe," meaning that excessive attention to these kinds of issues distracts us from the heart and depth of our message and its importance to the world. We must move beyond numbers so that our policies and practices of membership are shaped by a deeper and more meaningful commitment to our religious movement and not by a preoccupation with fundraising strategies.

The Question: When dealing with fundraising policies and practices, how do we best avoid obsession with the peripheral issues and get on with the business of growing strong congregations that take the message of our free, liberal faith to the world?

The Issue: Dual Membership

Many Unitarian Universalists belong to or attend more than one congregation on a regular basis. The most common situation is from the "sun birds" or "snow birds"—that is, people who summer or winter in another region of the country from their regular home. These congregations face many unique issues: counting part-time residents for the APF; determining a level of expected financial contribution; building budgets and raising funds to serve a congregation with peaks in participation; maintaining connections with part-year residents; and involving them in volunteer service in the congregation.

There are no simple answers to these questions, and to some degree each situation is unique. The question about the APF would simply disappear if a change from a per-member calculation for APF were adopted. The issues of promoting generous support for both congregations would remain. Other issues can best be resolved based on some basic principles.

We urge a broader conceptualization of membership that can help congregations address this issue. The connection of a person to the Unitarian Universalist movement ranges from visitor to church leader. A part-time resident may have a stronger connection to one congregation or the other, even though he/she is registered as a member in both. He/she may play different roles in each congregation. It is the connection to the congregation that is important, and focusing on a person's part-time status may weaken that connection by making people feel excluded.

In most of our congregations, the required financial contribution, if any, is minimal. We rely, as a matter of principle, on the individual or family unit to consider the financial needs of the congregation and their financial capability and to make a free decision about their giving. This is a matter of principle because, just as we respect each person's spiritual path, we respect their personal property. In each case, we avoid coercion. We suggest that the financial relationship between congregations and part-time members be handled in a similar way. Members must be made aware of the costs of providing services so that they can make appropriate financial commitments.

It is much the same with volunteer activities. Congregations can make a specific effort to organize their volunteer opportunities to accommodate the residential patterns of the members. Members can participate and make commitments even on a part-time basis. In recent years, people in many congregations are often less willing to make long-term commitments to committee work, and so congregations have tried to use shorter term task forces. This response is also suitable for part-time residents, allowing them to share their talents and experience in meaningful ways despite their regular absences from the congregational community. Dual membership does not have to be an "either/or" proposition.

In this regard, one dimension of membership that has not been discussed thus far in the report pertains to what happens when a person moves from one

Dual membership does not have to be an "either/or" proposition.

location to another. Often, he/she looks for another UU congregation in the area. There is, however, no process for notifying a congregation that a member of another congregation has moved to the area. In other denominations there is a formal letter of transfer of membership. As each UU congregation controls its membership, such a process of transfer of membership would not conform with our polity. A letter of introduction, however, would make that person feel more welcome and might preserve that member's connection with the Unitarian Universalist movement. Such a communication could help address the confusion some congregations and members experience in regard to dual membership.

Issues of transfer of membership and affiliation with the larger movement are especially germane when it comes to youth and young adults in our movement. As young people move away from their home congregations to go to college or establish themselves in professions in other parts of the country, their connection to the movement is even more important. Some UU congregations, as a part of their ministry to youth and young adults, take explicit steps to help young people find and affiliate with a UU congregation where they will be relocating.

The Questions: How can congregations be encouraged to see dual members as welcome participants and resources instead of problems? How might congregations with a substantial incidence of dual membership work together to help an individual grow a deeper commitment to the movement and to both congregations? What are strategies to provide a connection with the larger UU movement for youth and young adults as they leave the home community?

The Issue: Increasing Membership Requirements

As part of the study on membership, the Commission met with Unitarian Universalists all over North America. Without fail, the issue of raising the "entry" and "maintenance" expectations as a way to grow commitment was brought up in our hearings. While most participants agreed that increased commitment and depth of membership is desirable, they did not necessarily agree about how to achieve it. UUs spoke of increasing required financial contribution as a condition of membership. Other UUs spoke of removing financial contribution as a condition of membership entirely. Some congregations require a meeting with the minister and/or a vote by the Board of Trustees. Others make no requirement except signing a membership book. In yet another approach, many congregations encourage and invite persons interested in affiliating with the congregation to participate in orientations, membership classes, and so forth but do not actually require such participation. The approaches taken by those who spoke with the Commission were as many and varied as the congregations themselves.

The Commission heard a slightly different perspective on this issue when we met in Canada. Representatives of Canadian congregations identified a cultural difference on this issue, saying, "We are slower to make the commitment but when we make it, we make it stronger." Some attribute this to a cultural norm in Canada that is less individualistic than is generally found in the United States. The high rate of Fair Share contributions of Canadian congregations to the Canadian Unitarian Council was given as one example of that deeper commitment.

Regardless of the specific requirements for formal membership, the Commission believes that congregations will benefit from instituting more intentional strategies to affirm the meaning of membership. We also believe that membership processes should address the fact that membership in the local congregation also includes a larger affiliation with the UU movement.

The Questions: Do explicit criteria for membership violate the premise of our free faith? Are such criteria congruent with the principles and purposes of the UUA? How can a congregation best maintain the "creative tension" needed to define effective boundaries? What benefit accrues to congregations that help members strengthen their sense of affiliation with the larger UU movement? Should members coming into membership from another UU congregation be expected to participate in orientation programs and other classes designed to deepen commitment, such as those offered as part of the path to membership?

The Issue: Exclusion from Membership

Exclusion from membership seems totally contradictory from the traditions and principles of our free faith. Yet many do feel excluded. Exclusion can be formal (or deliberate) or informal. Informal exclusion happens most often when norms and expectations are not explicit. They may be inexplicit because of the homogeneity of the congregation. For example, a congregation that is predominantly (if not exclusively) made up of people of a similar theological bent, class, or ethnic heritage can exclude people from the congregation unintentionally. Informal exclusion can occur as well because of the familiarity and general informality of the relationships among people in the congregation. Eager and warm greetings among regular participants in the congregation—for example, during the coffee hour—can lead to unintentional exclusion of visitors and newcomers.

Unintentional exclusion, however, is not limited to visitors on Sunday morning. It may be, in fact, more common with people who have become more familiar with the congregation but are not yet engaged. They are past needing a friendly greeting on Sunday morning, but they are not yet integrated into congregational life. Responses to a survey conducted by the Commission as part of our study reveal that most congregations struggle with the inclusion of people in the life of the congregation. Respondents spoke of ongoing efforts to engage people who are on the periphery and of friction and discomfort among long-time and relatively new members: "It takes time to really belong. There is some mistrust on the part of old-time members—i.e., 'newcomers don't know how we do it here.' " "Long-time members are hungry for new blood, yet there is real resistance to change which, of course, new folks bring."

Another dimension of informal exclusion is self-exclusion. Self-exclusion can take place when visitors, "seekers" if you will, find that a particular congregation is not what they were looking for in a faith community and choose to go elsewhere. Some self-exclusion can be indicative of good boundaries and clear norms and expectations. As one survey respondent said, "Those who don't fit in don't stay." Some self-exclusion, however, takes place because of non-welcoming behaviors on the part of the congregation. These informal excluding practices are of great concern for they turn away those who are perhaps UU by identification but cannot find their way into the life of the congregation. As a result, we are all diminished.

A systems perspective on exclusion looks at bringing those informal or inexplicit practices into greater awareness and on the role that deliberate or formal exclusion plays in defining the boundaries of the congregation. In its 1997 report *Interdependence*, the Commission on Appraisal recommended that congregations establish provisions in their bylaws for the exclusion from membership in cases where an individual's behavior threatens the congregation's well-being. Most congregations remove people from membership only in response to circumstances in which the member has stopped participating, most generally financially, in the life of the congregation. There has been growing interest, however, in the question of excluding persons whose behavior violates the basic expectations and norms of the community. Increasingly, our congregations are recognizing that "living in a community implies—no, requires—an agreement on fundamental values."[5] Behavior that threatens those values, in some cases, justifies exclusion from membership.

Some congregations have established procedures for involuntary exclusion from membership for destructive and threatening behavior. *InterConnections*, a UUA publication for lay leaders of UU congregations, addressed this issue in an article called "Handling Disruptive People: Policies That Ease the Strain." This is an example of boundary definition, whereby a congregation adopts specific policies for involuntary exclusion of a member. Rev. Ken Collier, who believes every congregation should have a policy addressing disruptive behavior, states, "Inevitably there will be these kinds of crises. It's really important to have thought through these issues before they occur."[6] Most often these policies permit expulsion of anyone, with due process, who becomes a perceived threat to safety, disrupts activities, or *diminishes the appeal of the congregation to potential and existing members.*

Behavior that threatens those values, in some cases, justifies exclusion from membership.

It may not be so difficult to reach agreement about the need to remove someone from membership for threatening others with physical harm or for fomenting loud and angry interruptions to the Sunday worship service. It is more difficult, however, to reach agreement about the criteria and procedures for doing so. Many congregations do not have procedures in place to deal with even the most obviously threatening and invasive behaviors. As a result, leadership must expend considerable time and anguish developing a fair, compassionate, and clear response while they are in the middle of the crisis. Many congregations have established guidelines and procedures regarding contact with children and youth by persons with a history of abuse or assault. Experience demonstrates, however, that this is not the case with most congregations. Is it not healthier to engage in the steps needed to clarify norms and expectations as a part of the congregation's ongoing programs and activities than to find ourselves in a position of reactivity to uncomfortable situations? The recommendation that congregations think about this and develop procedures ahead of time is good advice.

It is, however, a challenging and slippery slope to define activities that "diminish the appeal of the congregation to potential and existing members" as grounds for formal exclusion. One person's prophecy may be seen to diminish the appeal of the congregation to others. Our discussion later in this report will address questions of inclusion and our difficulties learning to live with discomfort in order to create a diverse and welcoming community. As important as it can be to have clear expectations and procedures to deal with such situations, it is equally important that the congregation carry on careful and thoughtful deliberation lest they exclude people whose voices bring richness and creativity to the conversation, even if they also bring discomfort. This is yet another example of the creative tension in which we believe we must live if we are to grow vital and healthy congregations.

What fundamental values are so central to the core of our Unitarian Universalist congregational life that to threaten them would justify formal exclusion from membership?

The Questions: What fundamental values are so central to the core of our Unitarian Universalist congregational life that to threaten them would justify formal exclusion from membership? What kinds of behaviors diminish the appeal of the congregation? What would it mean to a congregation to have a discussion of this issue as part of a process to define its center of gravity? What if the norms and expectations were to become more explicit rather than implicit?

We hope these questions have stimulated you to think about the process of growing members in your congregation. They are not the only questions. It is important to also challenge some of your beliefs and assumptions about the meaning of membership.

Notes

1. Loren B. Mead, *More Than Numbers: The Way Churches Grow* (Washington, DC: Alban Institute, 1993), 60.
2. Ibid., 60.
3. Ibid., 65.
4. Barbara Wells, "Path to Membership: A Philosophy for New Member Ministry."
5. Terrance Sims, "Decision Making in the Congregation" (paper for Starr King School for the Ministry, April 2000).
6. Ken Collier, "Handling Disruptive People: Policies That Ease the Strain," *InterConnections* (March/April 1998).

The Challenge of Incarnation

"There are seasons in human affairs," wrote William Ellery Channing, "when new depths seem to be broken up in the soul, when new wants are unfolded in multitudes, and a new and undefined good is thirsted for."[1]

We believe that such a season is upon us. The challenge lies in satisfying the thirst of the "multitudes" in each of our individual congregations. A thirst for what? *Sanctuary*—what Laura Cerwinske describes as a "place of order and tranquility, a retreat from the disharmony of the world"?[2] Unquestionably. Community? Undeniably.

Dr. Martin Luther King spoke of creating the "Beloved Community," putting God's word into action, creating, if you will, the commonwealth of God on earth. And Zen Master Hsin Tao tells us that "a genuine *Pure Land* (paradise) has never existed in some far-off place, but resides right now in the cultivation of every being's heart."

How we cultivate our own hearts, *in safe spaces, and in community with one another*, is at the center of the theologies informing the Unitarian Universalist theology of membership. These include a dimension of growth and outreach that embraces perspectives broader than our own personal ones. Harry Nelson Wieman calls it "creative interchange," Mary Hunt speaks of "embodiment," and liberation theologians write of critical reflection on the lived experience.

The crucial relationship between our environment and its inhabitants is central to incarnation, the transformation of the idea, the word, the belief, into action. This is the essence of our UU Principles and Purposes. Rather than emphasizing an afterlife, we stress that our work is here on earth. Loren Mead refers to this as a "this-worldly" theological orientation.

Although recognizing that the independence of individuals within our congregations—and the independence of congregations within the UUA—is basic, we nevertheless have words that help us to articulate the shared theological foundation of our faith. And the foremost statements of our common ground are the Principles of the UUA, as stated in the bylaws (Article II, Section C.2.1).

These Principles are not "deemed to infringe upon individual freedom of belief[,] which is inherent in the Universalist and Unitarian heritages[,] or to conflict with any statement of purpose, covenant or bond of union used by any society unless such is used as a creedal test" (Article II, Section C.2.4).

Over the centuries, Unitarian and Universalist congregations have established language (either in the form of covenantal statements, mission statements, or statements of purpose) that has been intended to provide a common core for the diversity of belief in the free church.[3]

The edict of Toleration of 1568, in which King John Sigismund of Transylvania granted freedom of religion to specific Christian traditions, was radical for its own time. Statements adopted by UU congregations have continually changed, as the understanding of what "freedom of belief" means has changed, and as congregations have grown beyond the Christian roots of both the Unitarian and Universalist movements. The evolution of language evident in mission statements and statements of principle reflects the changing vision of the ideal life in the local congregation. Our Principles express gratitude for religious pluralism and the inspiration to deepen our understanding and expand that vision.

The Ideal of Pluralism vs. the Reality of UU Congregations

The UU composer Ysaye Maria Barnwell, of the *a capella* group Sweet Honey in the Rock, challenges us in song to face some of our deepest fears and to heed some of our deepest yearnings:

> Would you harbor me?
> Would I harbor you?
> Would you harbor a Christian, a Muslim, a Jew, a heretic, convict or spy?
> Would you harbor a runaway woman or child, a poet, a prophet, a king?
>
> Would you harbor an exile or a refugee, a person living with AIDS?
> Would you harbor a Tubman, a Garrett, a Truth, a fugitive or a slave?
> Would you harbor a Haitian, Korean, or Czech, a lesbian or a gay?[4]

Our Unitarian Universalist faith asserts that we do harbor one another; our Principles assume that we do. *Would you harbor me?* We choose whom we harbor. *Would I harbor you?* We are poised, as a religious collective, to be accountable in our answering.

In conversations on the topic of membership that have taken place all around our continent, some UUs held that the important issues are those related to recruitment and retention of a membership base that corresponds to populations most nearly matching the demographic characteristics of the present membership. New members are welcome as long as they "fit in," but the movement should not shift from its traditional demographic base in order to attract and include those of different backgrounds.

In one such conversation, the participants (all white) were asked to state their vision of their congregations' futures. One woman stated that she had a vision of multiracial, multicultural congregations. Another woman looked startled and then made a gesture indicating that she thought such a vision was unrealistic or inappropriate.

While many UUs may overtly or covertly feel the same way, others believe that for our movement to fully develop its potential, we must broaden our base and include diverse populations of Beloved Community. As time has passed, our understanding of religious pluralism has expanded. In recent years, the Sources of our living tradition have been amended to reflect that expanded understanding. For the purposes of this discussion, the Commission is including all dimensions of life experience that find expression in our free faith: gender, race and culture, class, theology, political belief, sexual orientation. We have indeed changed the words!

Incarnation, however, calls us to put the words into action. While what we say reflects a vision of pluralism, our congregations are made up of human beings. And as human beings, no matter how deeply we share the vision of our movement, at times we are going to fall short of the mark. What *is* the reality in our congregational lives?

Incarnational growth is not about recruiting; it is about transforming perspective and awareness. "Membership," writes Renee-Noelle Felice, "is not something conferred upon one person by an already extant group of 'others,' but a covenant among individuals to become something new." But when the "covenant" is broken—or ignored—hearts become bruised.[5] One UU told the Commission,

> It is extremely frustrating when one encounters opposition both personally and institutionally from UUs who constantly state (in subtle and not so subtle ways!) that there is no place for a more expressive, passionate style of worship. By this I mean more than just a change in music. At times, I want to revel in applause, dance, and "holy" shouts of affirmation during a service. The cultural aspects of those who come from a Euro-Mediterranean background (in my case, Italian American), for which this expression is vitally important, are many times ignored in favor of the more

well-known and stereotyped Anglo-European approach of dispassionate detachment. Why can't we honor both as opposed to either/or?

The Commission received input from hundreds of Unitarian Universalists from all over North America in response to questions about the meaning of membership. While much of the discussion focused on aspects of growth identified by Mead (numeric, maturational, and organic), there was also considerable discussion of how we manifest incarnational growth, the ways in which we "walk the talk" of our vision.

Ultimately, it is in the congregations that our vision comes to life—or does not—as we have heard in some cases. No matter what is stated in the UUA's Principles and Purposes and in our bylaws, our congregations are at liberty (with very little limitation) to define the nature of religious life and expression. Though many people are attracted to us because of our public expressions of religious tolerance, opposition to oppression, and inclusion of diverse populations, what they find in practice does not always match the Principles we espouse.

The Commission's conversations with people who self-define as Unitarian Universalist but feel "left out" of their local congregations, lead to the inescapable conclusion that exclusion is indeed a problem. Ironically, congregations that espouse respect for the inherent dignity and worth of all beings nevertheless engage in behaviors that exclude some others who identify with that same Principle.

One respondent said,

> I cannot tell you how appalled I was when, as a visitor to a Unitarian Universalist church, one of the very few persons of color in the congregation was introduced to me as "our token Black." During the coffee hour I felt compelled to ask him how he felt about that comment. He replied, "Yes, yes. It cuts to the very core of my being. But this is where I worship. This is my spiritual home. I am no spring chicken. I am too old to start over."

The Commission received many such reports. For example,

- suggestions that an African American visitor to a UU congregation might feel more comfortable in the church down the street
- opposition to incorporation of neo-pagan and earth-centered rituals
- repeated ignoring of visitors week after week, leading to feelings of invisibility
- criticism and disapproval of sermons or worship services presenting theologies other than those shared by the preponderance of members, whether they are Christian or Humanist or have some other perspective

Though many people are attracted to us because of our public expressions, what they find in practice does not always match the Principles we espouse.

- reluctance on the part of ministers to preach from their personal theological orientations because of negative judgment on the part of congregants
- financial policies that imply an assumption of middle- or upper-class status
- overt expressions of racial, cultural, or gender prejudice
- suggestions that if one is a Christian (or Humanist or Pagan, etc.) he/she doesn't belong in *this* congregation
- resistance to incorporating different cultural or language experiences into worship services
- assumptions that people of different classes, cultural groups, or ethnic backgrounds would not be attracted by the UU Principles

While many of our congregations have made notable progress in including gay men and lesbians into the mainstream of congregational life, inclusion of bisexual and transgender persons is another matter. One individual, a self-described "out" transgender person who met with the Commission, put it like this: "We claim to be open, believe in universal salvation, yet we cringe when transgender people come into our congregations. When I sing that 'I am singing for my life' I mean it. It's not safe to be transgender in this society."

Our conversations made it clear that numerous people who identify with Unitarian Universalist principles and values do not find strong support or welcome in their local congregations. It is now apparent to the Commission that many who resonate to UU theology or beliefs do not identify their congregations as their primary connections with the movement.

One person with whom the Commission talked spoke for many: "It's hard for me to sit in our congregations. I feel so completely invisible, calling myself a member is problematic. I cannot be fully who I am in a congregation."

Many with whom the Commission met spoke of the emotional sacrifice caused by maintaining their congregational connections. "Being a member of a congregation means nothing to me unless there is liberation," said another person. And yet another: "Until we achieve what the resolution [on Racial and Cultural Diversity] calls for, we will continue to give lip service to our desire to transform the world, and we will remain a mostly white, Euro-centric, monolingual, monocultural, middle-class religious movement [from] which many people of color will continue to feel culturally alienated." And someone else said, "I continue to be UU because religiously I cannot be anything else. I cannot do it, but there is a piece that is missing. When I need deep spiritual feeding, I go to the Spanish-speaking Catholic church."

These are voices of people who are committed to our vision. They serve as the voices of our congregations. They are telling stories that need to be heard. If we will but listen, their voices will help us all live deeper, more authentic, more creative lives.

The Need for Foundational, Not Cosmetic, Change

Poet Caroline Kandler writes,

> Here, I have some change.
> I have some quarters.
> Hey, I don't want your change.
> What I want is change—
> real change. . . .
> We want the changes that make room for us.[6]

If membership means a deepening of our commitment to the tending to our neighbors, in the sanctuaries of our own communities, then we must engage in the difficult conversations about whether and how our congregations promote *incarnational* growth.

Clearly, explicit as well as implicit barriers to membership exist. But each of us, as an individual, has boundaries that can be extended. So, too, do our churches. Those of us whose profiles do not match those of the majority of church members are not looking for small adjustments or concessions. We are looking for foundational changes in the culture of our institutions, changes that will allow us to be present with one another in new, healthy, and holy ways.

Diversity and *inclusion* are issues critical to who we are. By *diversity*, we mean that there are many voices to be heard—voices informed by racial, social, psychological, physical, cultural, and religious experiences. Creating the space for required listening can produce a new awareness, stimulate a new reaction, and give rise to a new sense of community based on its commitment to its shared vision. But it can also give rise to the uncomfortable recognition that *inclusion* means we have to share the deep and vulnerable parts of ourselves with others who are not quite like us; whose gender or race, physical characteristics, religious beliefs, or gender preferences make us squirm.

"One of the truths of our time," writes Mary Caroline Richards, "is this hunger deep in people all over the planet for coming into relationship with each other."[7] That is what brings us to the table—that yearning for community, the great desire to find others of like mind, the pursuit of spiritual deepening. And in the first flush of excitement at having found kindred spirits, it might seem as if there is only one kind of person at the table. Yet all too soon we realize that in the words of a popular hymn—sung most often when we celebrate the diversity espoused in our Principles and Purposes—there are, in reality, all kinds of people around the table. But when asked to dig deeper, this affirmation of difference quickly dissipates as our individual characteristics not only become evident, but threaten to separate us. The religious instruction (or lack thereof) that we received as children, the languages in which our par-

We are looking for foundational changes in the culture of our institutions, changes that will allow us to be present in new, healthy, and holy ways.

ents and grandparents spoke to us, our choices of life partners, our racial makeup, and our varying physical and mental abilities all combine to make us very different from one another. Thus, the challenge that lies before us is to find a way for all of us—some of us omnivores, some vegetarians, and even a few vegans—to stay at the table and be nourished.

The Hard Work Required to Make Change Happen

In Genesis 11:1-9, we read that "the whole world had one language and the same words."

> Now the whole earth had one language and the same words. And as they migrated from the east, they came upon a plain in the land of Shinar and settled there. And they said to one another, "Come, let us build ourselves a city, and a tower with its top in the heavens, and let us make a name for ourselves; otherwise we shall be scattered abroad upon the face of the whole earth." The Lord came down to see the city and the tower, which mortals had built. And the Lord said, "Look, they are one people, and they have all one language; and this is only the beginning of what they will do; nothing that they propose to do will now be impossible for them. Come, let us go down, and confuse their language there, so that they will not understand one another's speech." So the Lord scattered them abroad from there over the face of all the earth, and they left off building the city. Therefore it was called Babel, because there the Lord confused the language of all the earth.

Could this story have served, on some unconscious level, down through the ages, to support the concept of homogeneity? The people all spoke the same language and thus would become so powerful they could actually penetrate heaven. Therefore, having one language and one religion would make an empire impenetrable and allow its practitioners to get as close to heaven on earth as God would allow.

Of course, Unitarian Universalists advocate the principle that great truths lie in all religions. And most of us probably believe that paradise does not lie above the clouds. In fact, it is part of our unofficial credo that if we use our resources to surmount barriers rather than to erect them, we will achieve heaven on earth. We hold what Toni Morrison calls a "complicated, demanding . . . view of heaven as life; not heaven as past life."[8]

The complicated, demanding part, of course, is that in order to break down barriers, or to resist building them, we have to do the messy, difficult, and occasionally heart-wrenching work of acknowledging the worthiness of all beings, not just the ones who "speak the same language" we do.

Rev. Mark Morrison-Reed concedes that change is difficult, not just for those who feel marginalized, but also for those who are not quite ready to put the old table out with the trash. Yet he offers compelling reasons to move through the fear and resistance:

> To move forward as a denomination, we need first to ask ourselves why. I think there is only one authentic answer. For yourself. For yourself because you will feel more comfortable in a multicultural, multiracial congregation. For yourself because being part of an inclusive movement is more consonant with the self-image you hold of yourself as a religious liberal. For yourself so that the piece of you [that] feels guilty or angry about what "we aren't" can stop feeling guilty and let go of the anger. For yourself because you want the whole world to know about liberal religion. For yourself because you want a style of worship that strikes deeper spiritual [chords]. For yourself, not because you should, but because you yearn to be different. Not for them but for yourself—ourselves.[9]

Echoing Morrison-Reed, one person told the Commission, "The goal should not be to 'recruit' people, but rather for our congregations to understand the Latino culture and perhaps help community organizations. Why? . . . we do this for ourselves."

The Commission maintains that our theology of membership requires us to address the issues raised by the UUs who so candidly and courageously "spoke truth to power." It requires us to reduce and eliminate the barriers that threaten our ability to truly live our faith in the world.

Of course, we must be wary of letting the desire for a "politically correct" membership cloud our vision and lead us to invite newcomers in only to abandon them. The act of signing a membership book does not guarantee the elusive yet equitable sense of "ownership"—of belonging—that comes when a person truly feels welcomed into membership because of the gifts he/she brings, not because that individual's presence means increased numbers on the congregation's roster or one more substantial contribution to the coffers, or because her/his skin color or physical disability will salve the congregation's guilt over the homogeneous character of its membership.

As it stands today, in more congregations than not, if we welcome a person who is a minority of one (or two)—whether gay or disabled or more theocentric than the rest of us, for example—and he/she becomes an established member of the community, we cannot help but think that that person has "hung in there" with "all the rest of us" (different) congregants. If that person leaves, we can tell ourselves that she/he didn't really fit in. She/he will probably be more comfortable with her/his "own kind." Thus, we exonerate ourselves from the hard work of creating and re-creating community as each new individual broadens and strengthens our circle.

We would avoid some pitfalls if, instead of talking about growth and membership and outreach, we talk about creating sanctuary. If we work as hard—or harder—at creating safe and worshipful places as we do at creating diverse congregations, we will most likely find that, paradoxically, transforming the awareness of the congregation will result in changing its demographics. As one African American UU put it, "If you do [anti-racism work] and you don't attract persons of color, you're probably not really doing the work. Any effort to transform our movement will succeed or fail on the local level."

Accountability

A number of years ago, a young gay man was considering whether or not to join a congregation that had not yet affirmed same-sex marriage. After some time, he did apply for membership. "I realized," he said, "that I could wait for 'them' to do what I wanted them to do, or I could join, and help 'us' to move forward." In taking this step, he was holding both himself *and* the congregation accountable.

As persons of faith we should be deeply concerned with the spiritual well-being of our congregations. That concern *could* give rise to a stronger sense of community, one that might even precipitate an enhanced, vibrant relationship with those outside the walls of our own congregations. But for that to happen, we will have to fearlessly examine our attitude toward those excluded from power *within* our ranks. And for *that* to happen, we first have to recognize and confront the fact that such exclusion does exist.

True appreciation of diversity can only be achieved if we stay engaged. We must admit to ourselves and to one another that the issue of individual vs. institutional accountability in policy and structure can trigger as much discomfort, distress, and dissension as age, sexual orientation, race, ethnicity, socioeconomic status, and political views. Paying attention to our own feelings of dis-ease can help us avoid falling into such pitfalls as lack of respect for difference, ignorance, and inertia.

But let us be clear: We not only need to establish institutional mechanisms that hold the dominant culture accountable but each of us needs to stand up to those who would make us "less than" others. For instance, when a member of one congregation left her congregation, never to return, it was whispered about that a congregation officer had told the congregant in private conversation that there was no place there for the woman's vocal concern about gun violence; that to raise this issue was not appropriate.

If, indeed, the woman left because of the reputed conversation, then the official's words were the "operative trigger" of the departure. However, the congregant must also take some responsibility for allowing herself to be excluded from the life of the congregation. *When we let the power structure win with-*

out a fight, we are collaborating in the system. But no matter how much of a stand those of us who dwell on the margins of congregational life take, the active participation of those in power is necessary to bring about the kinds of institutional changes required.

Some years ago, a white woman, concerned for and passionately dedicated to helping abused women, was invited by another member of her denomination to attend a weekend conference linking sexism and racism. With all the goodwill in the world, the woman replied, "Racism isn't my issue," meaning that, while she supported efforts for racial justice, she didn't see it as her own personal ministry.

Not so, would argue a priest of African American descent, who has devoted his life to social justice work. Applauding the decision of a white acquaintance to attend a UU anti-racist workshop, he spoke at some length about the responsibility of members of the "dominant culture" to alter that culture; to build a table large enough, accessible enough, and sturdy enough to seat *all* of us.

History abounds with myriad—often horrific—stories of what can happen when members of the dominant culture dig in their heels and refuse to seat "outsiders" at their table.

A poignant example can be found in our own history. In the late 1800s Rev. Jenkin Lloyd Jones, as general secretary of the Western Unitarian Conference, opened the door to Unitarian women by inviting Rev. Mary Augusta Safford to co-found a church in Hamilton, Illinois. She became the "mother" of the Iowa Sisterhood, a group of approximately twenty women ministers who literally changed the face of Unitarianism. The Sisterhood founded fifteen churches, designing some of the buildings themselves. They preached and ministered, ran the Sunday schools, and established self-improvement groups. Universalists, too, at that time, had begun opening their pulpits to women. By 1890 there were seventy ordained female Unitarian and Universalist ministers.

Enter Rev. Samuel Eliot, president of the American Unitarian Association from 1900 to 1927. Almost immediately upon taking office, Eliot not only closed the door to women but he *locked* it! Rather than encouraging more women to assume pulpits, he began the promotion of a "manlier ministry." Adding insult to injury, Eliot invited leading Boston laymen and "prominent ministers' wives and alliance officers" to wait on tables at luncheons arranged "for the men" at the annual meetings, and started an (unsuccessful) school to train women to be parish assistants. Because of this attitude as well as other cultural/economic factors, by the time of the merger of the Universalist Church of America and the American Unitarian Association in 1961, there were very few women in the ministry.

Cynthia Grant Tucker tells us, "Frustrated by the laity's failure to take their sermons to heart, and weary of being anathematized by an institution that wanted them out, the clergywomen reluctantly shifted their ministry to the secular fields of settlement work, municipal housekeeping, suffrage, and world peace."[10] The moral of this tale is that no matter how assertive members of a particular group might be, their solitary efforts will not take them very far.

Programs created by the UUA and by individual congregations suggest that, perhaps for the first time in our history, there could be a paradigm shift. Rather than "letting" marginalized or minority people sit at "our" table, we are recognizing the need for *all members* of the congregation to work together to redesign the table.

Looking to the Past for Strength and Inspiration

One of the many gifts of Unitarian Universalism is that our different ways of thinking inform who we are. But this sometimes seems to be more bane than blessing. Like those long ago Israelites building a tower to heaven, we are discouraged by our inability to understand one another.

It is all too easy to forget that ours is a long walk to freedom. But consider the convictions of some of our standard bearers: Michael Servetus, Olympia Brown, John Murray, Julia Ward Howe, James Reeb, Whitney Young (to name a very few). All these were "heretics" who felt led to leave the main highway and strike off on their own on roads fraught with danger and even death. Yet they did not return to the safety of the straight and narrow once it became clear that they were on perilous paths.

Our path, too, often seems treacherous. On a journey fueled only by our faith and tenacity, we find that looking back over our shoulders at the past can sometimes help us to face the road ahead. As Harry Scholefield and Paul Sawyer remind us, "Discovering the depth and strength of these roots of ours is a nourishing experience that gives us the inspiration and stamina we need to meet today's great challenges."[11] Whether we give it voice or not, diversity is present. What matters is that we take concrete steps to acknowledge and celebrate that presence. As members of a choir strive to have their individual voices blend, so together we strive to be in harmony with one another. We may not always hit the right notes, and we sometimes have trouble hearing one another's voices, but the potential for making a truly joyful noise keeps many from looking elsewhere for a spiritual home.

Looking to the Future with Faith and Hope

To help ourselves lift up the themes around which we will weave our harmonies and variations, we create mission statements. Mission statements give voice to our visions, and embody the spirit of our congregational life. Yet in creating mission statements, we must ask ourselves what diversity will do for us. How will it help us build and sustain community?

Remarking on the focus on diversity for diversity's sake, Bruce Bush, a member of another liberal religious tradition, has written that, " 'diversity' is a red herring. The search for it is not ultimately freeing but condescending and patronizing...[and] seeks to impose our own progressive values on what should be a free society....What does it matter whether there are actually many 'diverse' individuals among us?"[12]

We believe that diversity matters a great deal. When all, or most, of us have more or less the same perspective on matters, we can only do so much to change our small portions of the world for the better. The greater the variety of perspectives, the more likely we are to come up with creative solutions to congregational and societal ills.

The process of creating our mission statements affords us a tremendous opportunity to examine who we are and what is of worth to us. If we make honoring diversity the bedrock of our statements, we will collectively widen our boundaries and create the safe spaces from which we can welcome those who could bring us the very points of view we might sorely need. For those who dare to venture off the beaten path, into the unknown, the reward is worth the risk: community and *sanctuary*, "a place to be creative, to seek meaning in life, to do the work of transformation that, at times, calls for descent into pain and chaos...a safe place to dance with the devil, to embrace lurking shadows on hallowed ground."[13]

Notes

1. William Ellery Channing as quoted in Carole Kammen and Jodi Gold, *Call to Connection: Bringing Sacred Tribal Values Into Modern Life* (Salt Lake City, UT: Commune-a-Key Publishing, 1998), 27.
2. Laura Cerwinske, *In a Spiritual Style: The Home as Sanctuary* (New York: Thames & Hudson, 1998), 22.
3. The importance of articulating that core is explored in depth in Walter P. Herz, ed., *Redeeming Time* (Boston: Skinner House Books, 1998).
4. Ysaye M. Barnwell, "Would You Harbor Me?" (Washington, DC: Barnwell Notes Publishing, 1994).
5. Renee-Noelle Felice, " 'Marrying' the Meeting," *Friends Journal* (April 1995): 17.
6. Caroline Kandler, "Changes."
7. Mary Caroline Richards, as quoted in Kammen and Gold, op. cit.
8. Toni Morrison, Nobel Lecture, 1993.
9. Mark D. Morrison-Reed, *Black Pioneers in a White Denomination*, 3rd ed. (Boston: Skinner House Books, 1994), 210.
10. Cynthia Grant Tucker, *Prophetic Sisterhood: Liberal Women Ministers of the Frontier, 1880-1930* (Bloomington: Indiana University Press, 1994), 6.

11. Harry Scholefield and Paul Sawyer, "Our Roots" in *The Unitarian Universalist Pocket Guide*, 3rd ed., edited by John A. Buehrens (Boston: Skinner House Books, 1999), 71.
12. Bruce Bush, "The Fine Line of Diversity," *Friends Journal* (October 1996): 18.
13. Cerwinske, op. cit., 22.

Pathways to Growth

In the very distant past, people attended the only church in their community. The choice was to attend or not, not which religion to be affiliated with. The changes over the centuries and through the generations have altered this, and now there are multiple paths to a religious community. People still seek out the church around the corner, but they also seek out interest groups, support groups, websites, recommendations of friends and families, and many other routes to congregational involvement. Young people find Unitarian Universalism through youth or young adult groups, those of differing religious identities find UUism through covenant groups, activists find UUism through involvement in social justice programs, etc. Our camps and conference centers, our involvement in the community, our willingness to welcome and embrace a diversity of people mean that people find our religious movement through non-traditional routes.

Numerous people who are not legal members of congregations consistently report themselves to be UUs through polling, survey, and census data. Many who identify as UUs and are not involved in our congregations are involved in some of the extra-congregational organizations within the Unitarian Universalist movement. And many who are involved find themselves more comfortably at home within these extra-congregational organizations. The extra-congregational routes to involvement provide opportunities to expand and share Unitarian Universalism and to strengthen individual commitment to Unitarian Universalism. No longer is affiliation with a member congregation of the Unitarian Universalist Association the only way that people identify themselves as Unitarian Universalists or live out UU loyalty and commitment (if it ever was!). Nor are UU congregations the only way in which our tradition is supported and lived out in the greater community.

Yet as a congregationally based Association, it has sometimes been difficult to understand the way in which extra-congregational affiliation fits within our system of congregational polity, and sometimes even the mere presence of these extra-congregational organizations creates tensions. Questions arise about competing loyalties to the congregation and to the extra-congregational organization, who is welcome in the congregation, how the corporate body reacts to the presence of extra-congregational groups within its sphere, who controls the agenda of the congregation, and how responsive the congregation is to a diversity of needs and concerns. The seeming polarities created by the existence of people who are more closely tied to extra-congregational associations can end up being agents of creative change. Extra-congregational organizations provide some people with a UU context, a greater sense of belonging that they have not found within our congregations, and a deepening of their already strong congregational identity.

It has sometimes been difficult to understand the way in which extra-congregational affiliation fits within our system of congregational polity.

What Are Extra-congregational Organizations?

By extra-congregational organizations, we refer to the official and unofficial UU-related, non-congregational bodies. Non-congregational organizations include several different types of organizations. They include groups at the cluster and district level, but more relevant to this report are the Associate Member and Independent Affiliate organizations. The UUA bylaws make provisions for both Associate[1] and Independent Affiliate[2] organizations. Some of these Associate and Independent Affiliate organizations are membership-based organizations, and several have groups either in local congregations, at the district level, or both. The list of organizations that are, and are not, either Associate or Independent Affiliate organizations fluctuates, based primarily on whether or not the groups have filed the requested information with the UUA and been subsequently approved by the UUA's Board of Trustees. For purposes of this report, these are referred to as unofficial organizations, with no slight intended but rather in reference to their affiliation with the UUA as an institution at this particular time.

Some of these Associate, Independent Affiliate, and unofficial organizations require affiliation with a UU congregation for membership (most notably the professional organizations), but most of these organizations do not. It is almost impossible to say whether or not the majority of the Associate and Affiliate groups' members see their participation in these groups as an augmentation to their congregational involvement or whether it is an alternative to congregational life. Rather, individuals may seek out these organizations as entry points or end points of association with Unitarian Universalism. Associate, Independent Affiliate, and unofficial groups provide an introduction to our values and to the things UUs care about and provide a way for easing out of the movement when Sunday morning activities no longer serve a purpose.

For many others, however, these organizations are an outgrowth and continuation of their UU involvement. They are a way to focus on a particular topic (such as with social justice-based organizations) or to obtain support around a particular identity (DRUUMM, Latino/a UU Networking Association, Interweave, as examples). These groups offer places to interact with others who have similar opinions or identities, especially for those of us who are in the minority in our local congregations.

For others, participation in these organizations is their only UU participation, and for some of these, the fact that the organization is UU-related and/or identified is insignificant—it is the program or people that draws them, not the religious label. This can be especially true for those involved in camps and conferences and in our youth and young adult movements.

The nature of these involvements creates tensions, simply by the fact that for some individuals, their affiliation with the extra-congregational organization pulls them away from congregational life, while for other individuals, it strengthens their congregational ties. In some congregations, the struggle over congregational identity is heightened by the presence of these organizations and there is seen to be competition for the right to define the congregation, while in other congregations, the presence of diverse groups strengthens the desire for diversity.

The nature of these involvements creates tensions.

Extra-congregational Organizations' Experiences

To gain greater understanding of the role of extra-congregational organizations within the UUA, and to understand the tensions better, the Commission met with representatives from several extra-congregational organizations during the 1999 General Assembly. Knowing we could not meet with all the existing organizations, we chose a subset that we believed would give us a broader understanding of membership questions and issues. Clearly, all those in the focus groups were also actively involved in congregational and the Association's life, or they would not have been at the General Assembly. As well, many were ministers and thus had a high degree of connection and commitment to the congregational base of the UUA. However, in speaking with the Commissioners, they spoke not only of their personal experience but of the experience of other members of their groups who were not connected with congregational life.[3]

Theological/Religious Extra-congregational Organizations

For those involved in the various theological/religious extra-congregational organizations, this extra-congregational association strongly supports their involvement in local congregations and, in some cases, provides them with a vehicle for continued association with Unitarian Universalism outside of the congregational structure. Currently, there are five theological/religious extra-congregational organizations associated with Unitarian Universalism: Covenant of UU Pagans (CUUPS), Friends of Religious Humanism (FRH), UU Buddhist Fellowship (UUBF), UU Christian Fellowship (UUCF), and UUs for Jewish Awareness (UUJA).

UUCF and FRH differ from the other three theological extra-congregational organizations in that either in the past or currently the theological approach they advocate was or is the dominant theology of Unitarianism, Universalism, and/or Unitarian Universalism. Both Unitarianism and Universalism originated as part of the Christian tradition, and it was not until the middle of the twentieth century, with the rise of the Humanist movement, that individuals, let alone congregations, began to seriously question Christianity as a shared theological understanding. By the end of the twentieth century, a large proportion of our congregations was primarily Humanist in outlook.

On the other hand, the theological orientations represented in CUUPS, UUBF, and UUJA have not had that level of popular support and understanding in our congregations. Although CUUPS boasts the largest membership of any of these groups, only 1 percent of our congregational membership is involved in CUUPS. A survey done by CUUPS in the late 1990s found that 85 to 90 percent of its members were currently either members or pledging friends of UU congregations. This survey represents only those who were official members of the continental body, and there are many people who, while they may claim CUUPS membership, are members of local chapters and may not be otherwise affiliated with the continental body or with Unitarian Universalism. Despite its relative newness in the pagan world (organized in 1985), it is one of the larger pagan organizations in the United States. For a chapter to be accepted into the organization, it must have at least three officers who are both members of a UU society and members of CUUPS.

UUJA is comprised primarily of individuals who grew up either culturally or religiously as Jews and who have made their religious homes since that time in UU congregations. Many within this group are (or were) in interfaith marriages and sought a theological middle ground that would honor both traditions. UUBF, the newest of these groups, has only twenty local groups meeting throughout the continent. In order to be identified as a UU Buddhist practice group, UUBF requires the groups to have strong affiliation with a local congregation.

For UU Christians, the existence of UUCF offers support and resources for Christians within our congregations. Although the predominant worship style in UU congregations follows the Reform Christian format (readings, hymns, sermon, with the sermon as the focal point of the service), many UU Christians do not feel affirmed in the worship. For them, Jesus and a liberal interpretation of the Christian Bible are important parts of their individual theologies, and they find that, depending on their local congregation, this is rarely supported. (This is not true in the New England congregations that have retained much of their association with Christianity but it is held to be so by those UU Christians outside of predominantly Christian congregations.) As one member of the focus group stated, "I wouldn't be a UU anymore if it wasn't for UUCF. By maintaining a Christian presence in the UUA it makes it possible for me to be a Christian and a UU. Christians are marginalized in the UUA." Another participant stated that he is involved in "a pluralistic church" and that he "stays somewhat closeted about his Christian theology." UUCF allows him to express his "theological nature even if it is truncated" in his local congregation. The spirit of the teachings of Jesus is there, but as a minister, he "dechristian-izes" the language.

Similar stories are told by those who are Humanist. Many Humanists have an abiding sense that the movement is losing its way in the recent swing toward the inclusion of more spiritual, religious language in programming at both the local and the continental levels. Gatherings of FRH at recent General Assemblies have spent time considering the nature of the shift in theological language. Many feel that they are in the process of losing their religious homes. They believe that Unitarian Universalism is moving away from its place in the theological/religious world and becoming very much like other liberal Christian communities. FRH strives to keep a Humanist stance alive and accepted within our UU congregations.

Many feel that they are in the process of losing their religious homes.

UUCF and FRH are united in their belief that congregational life should reflect their particular theological outlook, at least part of the time. Members of both organizations expect to hear language that reflects their theologies in services and in the music and readings. While the atheist Humanists bewail the addition of spirituality and "god-talk," the Christians appreciate the inclusion but often long for explicitly Christian language and readings. There is an inherent tension in these requests: For Humanists and Christians alike, the ideal worship community would offer language that evokes their imagery and beliefs, without need of translation. However, it is a logical impossibility to use the language of both groups within the same service. One either uses language that includes Jesus or does not; there is no middle ground except for long-term balance.

Members of CUUPS long for imagery that evokes the goddess and earth-centered spirituality. Pagan UUs seek out CUUPS on a continental and local level in order to find worship that is most meaningful to them. Although many of our congregations now celebrate some of the neo-pagan festivals and holy days (most notably the solstices and equinoxes), very few, if any, congregations are focused primarily around goddess and earth-centered spirituality, despite the addition of the sixth Source to the UUA's Statement of Principles.[4] CUUPS provides an outlet and place of worship for many who identify with the neo-pagan movement.

UU Buddhists do not, by and large, expect the worship services of their local congregations to be primarily Buddhist in orientation. For Western Buddhists, there is no established community of worshippers, and so those who seek religious community must find it outside of their Buddhism. As one Buddhist says, "Unitarian Universalism is culturally Christian (the metaphoric framework is Christian), carries rationalist and nineteenth-century humanist values (the liberal impulses in Christianity), and it also honors my Buddhism. It challenges and questions me. I feel that Buddhism is not marginalized, but at the center of lived UUism."

Jewish UUs do not expect worship to be predominantly Jewish in nature, but they prefer that the worship not be exclusively Christian either. Many find it difficult to associate with something called a *church* and would prefer other names such as *congregation, fellowship,* or *society.* As well, many culturally Jewish UUs find support for the celebration of Jewish holidays and holy days, such as Pesach, Hanukkah, Rosh Hashanah, and Yom Kippur in their UU congregations, especially in cities with a larger proportion of Jews. This acknowledgement, along with the blending of various religious approaches for those who are in interfaith marriages, is an important part of their involvement within a UU congregation.

Reactions to the existence of these groups within congregations varies widely. Some congregations provide support for these extra-congregational organizations and find that the variety of theological services provided by these organizations supplements what occurs on Sunday mornings. Other congregations prohibit, by custom or directive, the activities of these groups and the diversity of worship style they bring to our movement. We heard of several congregations that do not allow CUUPS chapters to use their buildings or hold their worship services in the congregational buildings, in some cases even when the members of the chapter are members of the local congregation.

Extra-congregational Organizations Based on Ethnic and/or Racial Identity

Although the UUA is and has been firmly committed to civil rights for persons of color and those of differing ethnic backgrounds, there have often been strong disagreements about what this means within the Association and how best to achieve and practice an openness to non-European Americans.[5] Since the early to mid-1990s, the Association has taken on the goal of becoming an anti-racist organization that strives to be open to people of various racial and ethnic diversities.

However, as the journey has not always been easy, members of various racial and ethnic minorities have created Affiliate organizations to provide support and counsel in the process of the UUA's transformation. The most recent of these organizations are UU Network on Indigenous Affairs (UUNIA), Diverse Revolutionary UU Multicultural Ministries (DRUUMM), and Latino/a UU Networking Association (LUUNA). African American UU Ministers (AAUUM) helped found DRUUMM, and it no longer exists as a separate organization.

DRUUMM and LUUNA (and formerly AAUUM) provide safe and supportive places for persons of color and differing ethnic groups within our Association. Members of the focus group explained their involvement in these organizations this way:

- "AAUUM provided a place for African Americans to meet, share concerns that only applied to them. It also was a safe place where I could say things that might not be understood elsewhere. That helped me stay with the UUA. It filled gaps that the congregation did not meet."
- "On a personal level, the congregation has been important to me...the sense of community. At the level of LUUNA, it supplements the involvement at the congregational level. It's a way of working on important projects; it's fun and comradeship. There's probably not a UU church that has a half-dozen Latinos in the country."
- "As an Indian person whose ancestors have been oppressed and exploited by organized religion, joining a church was probably the last thing I wanted to do. A professor said the UUA is 'not that bad,' not really much of a church at all, good people, inclusive, it'll work....I found UUNIA at General Assembly, 'thank God.' It's very much a reason why I have stayed through thick and thin. It's hard for me to sit in our congregations. I feel so completely invisible, calling myself a member is problematic....There is a home for me with these groups [UUNIA], but not in a congregation. I cannot be fully who I am in a congregation."

For most, their involvement in UUNIA, AAUUM, DRUUMM, and LUUNA are important parts of their involvement in Unitarian Universalism, and for many these organizations are their primary loyalty and community of nurture and support. For some, their participation in Affiliate organizations is the only thing that keeps them in Unitarian Universalism, for through these groups they link up with others who share their identity and are committed to ensuring that the UUA becomes (and then remains) an anti-racist organization.

These groups have served almost as political action groups within the UUA to push for equality of all, regardless of racial or ethnic definition. AAUUM began both to offer support to African American ministers, as well as to lobby

For some, their participation in Affiliate organizations the only thing that keeps them in Unitarian Universalism.

with the Department of Ministry for those ministers who experienced difficulty getting into Fellowship and into congregations once in Fellowship. DRUUMM has worked within the UU Ministers' Association to make sure that issues of concern to ministers from various minorities are raised and dealt with and to help further the UUMA in its goal of becoming anti-racist. LUUNA has worked to ensure that material is available in Spanish for individuals who may be interested in Unitarian Universalism.

The majority of the members of these organizations are also involved in local congregational life, though the degree of individual involvement varies greatly (as it does for individuals who are not members of extra-congregational associations). However, many still feel marginal or invisible in their congregations. Frequently, these individuals are also expected to bear the burden of explaining themselves and justifying their existence within the congregation to other congregational members.

The tensions felt in congregational life for members of these groups are similar to tensions arising from differing theological orientations, primarily the questions of who gets to define the culture of the congregation and the amount of diversity in style of worship and other programmatic areas of congregational life. Again, some congregations have found the presence of these groups supportive of their efforts to provide greater racial/cultural diversity, whereas others believe the existence of these groups provides unfair political pressure on the congregations.

Extra-congregational Organizations Based on Sexual Orientation and Gender

Interweave (formerly Unitarian Universalists for Lesbian, Gay, and Bisexual Concerns) was originally created in 1971, and was revived in the early 1980s. It works alongside the UUA's Office of Bisexual, Gay, Lesbian, and Transgender Concerns (OBGLTC) to promote the support and inclusion of bisexual, gay, lesbian, and transgender UUs within our congregations and in society as a whole. It was through the work of Interweave and OBGLTC that the curriculum *The Welcoming Congregation*[6] and designation of Welcoming Congregation were created. Although early on this group was essential in forming a welcoming atmosphere within our congregations and ministry, by now the cultural and social changes in our congregations (with help from Interweave) and society at large have greatly changed for the better. As of July 27, 2000, 257 of our 1,032 congregations have received Welcoming Congregation status, and 200 to 300 more are in process.

During our focus group sessions, individuals expressed that it is often through Interweave involvement that individuals first feel fully free to be themselves within a religious context. Most members of the organization are ac-

Many still feel marginal or invisible in their congregations.

tively involved in their congregations and feel that they have been supported by the presence of Interweave. There is an understanding that Interweave and the OBGLTC have had a great impact in transforming our congregations, in a way that the anti-racism work has not yet done. Most, if not all, of our congregations have openly bisexual, gay, and lesbian members, and a large percentage of our bisexual, gay, lesbian, and transgender clergy are open about their sexual orientations. Whereas in the past being bisexual, gay, or lesbian made settlement in our congregations very difficult, problems in settlement have now become isolated cases. (The same cannot be said for the relatively small number of transgender ministers who have sought settlement. They still experience difficulty in the settlement process.)

Individuals mentioned that they still have strong ties to their local congregations, but there is often a sense of "coming home" when in groups of BGLT people. Additionally, it was noted that involvement in Interweave helped individuals tie in with other movements within the Association, such as anti-racism work and other social justice issues. It has brought an awareness of the larger UU world into their lives and helps them keep perspective.

However, tensions still exist within our congregations about the involvement of BGLT people. Some congregations are hesitant to be known as the "gay church" within their communities and urge a low-key approach and lack of advertising within the gay/lesbian community, whereas other congregations warmly embrace Interweave chapters as viable components of their membership, ministry, and outreach.

Yet another area in which the UU movement has made great strides over the past thirty-five years is in the area of women's rights and participation. The UU Women's Federation, founded in 1963 through the consolidation of the Association of Universalist Women (organized in 1869) and the Alliance of Unitarian Women (organized in 1890), was one of the major bodies through which lobbying and support of women in Unitarian Universalism happened. The UUWF brought many women to leadership in our movement, helped to challenge the language of our governing documents, and supported women in the ministry. UUWF, alongside the Women and Religion Task Force, worked to ensure that our bylaws, and most notably our Principles, were written in language that was inclusive of all people. These organizations also provided early support for Interweave through working collaboratively with them, and they helped to support women ministers as they sought parity in settlement and remuneration with their male colleagues. Like Interweave and BGLT individuals, UUWF helped transform the face of Unitarian Universalism, especially its ministry, to be more reflective of society at large.

For many women, involvement in UUWF has provided a depth to their involvement at the local congregational level and helped them achieve a sense of wholeness in their congregational lives. This has been through the transformation of governing structures and the increased use of female imagery, as well as

Interweave and the OBGLTC have had a great impact in transforming our congregations, in a way that the anti-racism work has not yet done.

the use of inclusive language. For some women, however, UU involvement is primarily through UUWF and its local and district chapters. There is still tension in some congregations over issues of inclusive language and over the various imageries used for the holy, but these tensions seem to have been greatly reduced over the past thirty years.

Political and Economic Extra-congregational Organizations

Whereas Unitarian Universalism clearly states that it has no theological creed, there are those who contend that we do have a political creed—that of liberal politics, most notably Democrat in the United States and New Democrat and Liberal within Canada. However, our members reflect a diversity of political beliefs. For every resolution or statement that is passed at General Assembly, there are people in the pews and pulpits who do not agree with it. Similarly, although several surveys report that the majority of Unitarian Universalists is middle-class, there are also some who are not and some who, regardless of their own class, work for economic justice and the inclusion of a broader class base within Unitarian Universalism.

There are those who contend we do have a political creed—that of liberal politics.

Two Independent Affiliate organizations were created to address the concerns and needs of these individuals within the UU movement. As described by the 1999 UUA Directory, the main purpose of Conservative Forum for UUs (CFUU) is to ensure that UUs "are free to pursue a responsible search for religious truth and meaning in our societies and denomination, regardless of individual views on politics, economics, or social issues."[7] The main purpose of UUs for a Just Economic Community (UUJEC) is "to focus our denomination's attention and power toward effecting systemic economic change that will serve the common good" and in particular toward a "theology of relinquishment."[8]

These membership-based groups are made up almost entirely of people who are members of local congregations, and these groups aim to support their members and to broaden the outlook and complexion of UU congregations. Believing that liberal religion is not restricted to those who are liberal politically, or in the economic middle class, these groups aim to transform and open up local UU congregations.

Camps and Conference Centers as Extra-congregational Organizations

Many find that UU camps and conference centers are their closest ties to organized Unitarian Universalism. A person active in both a UU congregation and a camp/conference center observes, "There's something about the way a camp community is formed that answers whatever seeking is under way." She adds that worship in nature is more meaningful to her than worship in a closed space. She speaks for many who choose to share their energies between a congregation and a camp/conference center—or who choose to participate in the life of a camp/conference only. A more direct connection with nature, with the outdoors and those who are drawn to it, attracts people to active participation in the life of camps and conferences. They feel part of a community with shared values and concerns that outweigh the differences they experience in other aspects of their lives, including within congregations. Church as community is very important to many who become members of congregations. It is equally important to those whose primary affiliation is with a camp/conference center.

A second respondent, a recent retiree and board member of the camp that he first attended as a child, expresses another view, also shared by others. He lives in a small city with a UU congregation, but he despairs of "church politics," citing the length of time to make and carry out decisions and the ill will that, for him, too often accompanies the process. He has no involvement with that congregation, describing himself as a "camp UU." A committed environmentalist, he goes to the camp when few others are there, thereby experiencing very little of human community but observing the impact of people on the camp's setting and working on policies and procedures to maintain its physical integrity. His identification combines his family's religious tradition with his personal commitment to the UUA's seventh Principle.

Both people independently emphasize the importance of camp experiences on the likelihood of young people's remaining involved Unitarian Universalists. One observed that "kids need rituals and formalities, and they develop these at camp," adding that young adults who stay with Unitarian Universalism through and after college often do so in a camp/conference context. Both remarked that, at camp, young people find a peer group and develop friendships in a unique, somewhat isolated context. They think this is especially true for young people from small and mid-size congregations who share an intense experience with similar youth and are involved in team building and empowerment perhaps for the first time. This kind of positive experience, focused expression of UU values, often provides a religious binding to Unitarian Universalism that doesn't happen—or happen to the same degree—in a congregational context.

For a retired couple, a camp/conference center became family in their retirement. They first saw and experienced the camp during a retreat sponsored by the UU congregation in their retirement city. For them, the binding was almost instant. They sold their home, bought another close to the camp/conference center, and became deeply involved in its life. They cite the beautiful setting, welcoming and appreciation of volunteers, and the warm, caring, and visionary staff. People who come to the camp tend to have different social, religious, and political views from most of their neighbors, so their comfort level is relatively high at the camp. In addition, all ages are welcomed and involved.

Thus, people involved with this center became family, especially since the couple's children lived several thousand miles away. This couple were members of a religious community and an extended family within one institution, and they supported it with time, energy, and money.

Mobile and volatile contemporary society leaves many people with unmet needs: for a sense of belonging; for the opportunity to give their time and talent and make a noticeable difference; for a smaller, more manageable space in which to live and reflect, even if only for a week or two; for others with whom to share thoughts and feelings in an atmosphere of trust and respect. Unitarian Universalist camps and conference centers provide a setting in which many people find at least some of these needs met, often especially those who have no other UU involvement. Some members find that camps and conference centers are good places to augment that which they receive from their congregational involvement. This can present the same sorts of tensions that are created by involvement in other extra-congregational organizations. Questions of higher loyalty and depth of commitment can be raised by those in the congregation who resent the camp or conference center involvement. Yet, these camps and conferences help cement some people more firmly within our UU movement, providing them a valid place to express their religious commitment.

Nonetheless, these camp communities, worlds within the greater UU world, are as subject to the effects of first disillusionment as are traditional congregations. There can be "bad marriages" between campers/participants and camp staff just as between congregations and ministers. People may not treat one another well. Loyalties can be strained. Willingness to overcome obstacles, to take the long view, to rate membership in these affiliate UU entities as more important than the disappointment, functions precisely as it does within congregations and fellowships. Survival of the institution, or of the membership, requires care, sensitivity, goodwill, and work on everyone's part. Religious institutions are no different from others in this regard. The human factor and relationships affect deeply how Unitarian Universalists value their memberships.

Is Tension a Problem or an Opportunity?

The majority of these extra-congregational organizations exist for two reasons: to support their members during their participation in local congregations and to transform the face of Unitarian Universalism. They see their role as being that of increasing and supporting the diversity in our movement and helping Unitarian Universalism live up to the promise of diversity encompassed in our non-creedal tradition committed to the inherent worth and dignity of every person. As such, they and their members must be taken seriously in any consideration of the meaning of membership within our Association and congregations.

As a movement that upholds and values diversity, it is incumbent upon congregations to provide welcome and hospitality to all those who are in agreement with our UU Principles, values, and traditions. Congregations have an affirmative responsibility to provide an atmosphere that is welcoming and encouraging of individual freedom of belief and conscience. There should be variety in the images and metaphors used; in the readings, music, and other worship components; and in the social and cultural life of the congregation.

However no one group, whether majority or minority, can expect an individual congregation to focus exclusively on its particular religious approach or identity. One aspect of the tension about diversity is a fear (sometimes well-founded) that our congregations and their resources will be taken over by groups whose missions and visions are not consistent with Unitarian Universalist traditions and values. Similarly, congregations fear that extra-congregational associations will become homes for the disillusioned, dissatisfied, angry membership that tries to undermine the overall health of congregational life without being in relationship. A balance must be strived for, despite the creative tension inherent in such a proposition. Extra-congregational associations must be deeply committed to the well-being of our institutional life as well as to the particularity of their individual foci. They must embrace the overall aims and intentions of our movement, and they have the responsibility to promote to their members responsible membership and participation in local congregations, consistent with our norm of democratic process. Extra-congregational groups should not set themselves up in adversarial positions or as power blocks to manipulate congregations, just as congregations should not use their power to block the existence of extra-congregational associations.

However no one group can expect an individual congregation to focus exclusively on its particular religious approach or identity.

Extra-congregational organizations and their local chapters should be welcome within our UU congregations, and congregations should support them in creating worship, educational, and social justice experiences that are of value to members of these organizations. Congregations should strive to educate themselves about the various needs, issues, concerns, and gifts that members of extra-congregational organizations can bring to the congregation and not rely simply upon members of these groups to do all the work to make deeper connections. If the challenge of mutual respect and responsibility is embraced by both congregations and extra-congregational associations alike, then each can serve to deepen the individual religious journeys and explorations of those involved in Unitarian Universalism and the tensions between the individual and the community can be held in a creative, not destructive, tension.

Notes

1. An Associate organization is an organization whose purposes and programs are "auxiliary to and supportive of the principles of the Association and

which pledges itself to support the Association" (Bylaws, Section C-3.7). These organizations are limited to "major continent-wide organizations," and a list of the current Associate organizations can be obtained from the UUA or found on the UUA's website, www.uua.org.

2. An Independent Affiliate organization is one whose purposes and intentions are "in sympathy with the principles of the Association" (Bylaws, Section C-3.8). Such status is for a one-year renewable term. The list of Independent Affiliates is fluid, based on whether the proper forms have been filed and approved by the UUA Board of Trustees. Some groups "disappear" for a year, and then return. A current listing of Independent Affiliates can be obtained from the UUA or found on the UUA's website, www.uua.org.

3. Groups invited to be part of the focus groups included UU Buddhist Fellowship, UU Christian Fellowship, Friends of Religious Humanism, Young Religious Unitarian Universalists, Continental UU Young Adult Network, Latino/a UU Networking Association, Diverse Revolutionary UU Multicultural Ministries, Urban Church Coalition, UUs for a Just Economic Community, Liberal Religious Educators Association, UU Ministers Association, Interweave, Council of UU Camps and Conferences, UU Women's Federation.

4. The sixth Source, "Spiritual teachings of Earth-centered traditions which celebrate the sacred circle of life and instruct us to live in harmony with the rhythms of nature," was added at the 1995 General Assembly.

5. Much of this history is captured in Commission on Appraisal, "Empowerment: One Denomination's Quest for Racial Justice, 1967–1982," available in *Unitarian Universalism and the Quest for Racial Justice* (Boston: Unitarian Universalist Association, 1993) and Mark Morrison-Reed, *How Open the Door? The Experience of Afro-Americans in Unitarian Universalism* (Boston: Unitarian Universalist Association, 1989).

6. UUA Office of Bisexual, Gay, Lesbian, and Transgender Concerns, *The Welcoming Congregation Handbook: Resources for Affirming Bisexual, Gay, Lesbian, and/or Transgender People*, 2nd ed. (Boston: Unitarian Universalist Association, 1999)

7. Unitarian Universalist Association, *UUA Directory, 1999-2000* (Boston: Unitarian Universalist Association, 1999), 401.

8. Ibid., 410.

Investing in Youth and Young Adults

One of the problematic areas of membership for many congregations is that of youth and young adults (age 18–35). There is a tension between wanting youth to be involved in the congregation and the need of youth for a healthy separation as part of their development. When can young people become members? How can children be recognized as members of the congregation community? Are young adults welcomed into leadership? Does membership in a district young adult group discourage membership in a congregation? In this chapter we will consider the application of the three categories described above (Identification, Affiliation, and Membership) to the situations of youth and young adults.

We say that young people represent the future of the church. However, we often push them to the periphery, rather than welcoming them into the congregation. Meg Muckenhoupt writes,

Here are the four easy steps to denominational death:

1. Separation—Gather together the most energetic, creative, socially conscious new members of your church in one big room. Let's call them the "Boosters." Tell them that they're special, wonderful people. Continue by telling them that they're so amazing that they have different needs from the rest of the congregation, which would be better

filled by meeting with other Boosters than bothering with the rest of the church.

2. Isolation—Arrange for the Boosters to have their own meetings at times when no one else is in the building. Encourage them to take on new leadership roles and responsibilities but only in groups made up entirely of Boosters. Casually mention that non-Booster committees are "boring" and "don't get anything done."

3. Disaffection—Lead small-group services where each Booster gets to talk about his or her own problems, but isn't required to respond to what anyone else has to say. They'll get used to concentrating on themselves instead of learning how to listen and worship as part of a congregation. If a few of the Boosters do sneak off and attend the regular Sunday-morning service, they'll complain that the service is "boring" and "doesn't speak to me," and leave.

4. Rejection—After the Boosters have been meeting for a few years, tell them that they can no longer use the church. Do not invite them to New U classes. Let them find their own heartbroken way back—they will if they're *really* UU, after all.

The scheme is guaranteed to be effective. After a few years, only weary refugees from other religions will be left in your church—hardly a group that can maintain its numbers, much less threaten the right-thinking world with a liberal faith.

There's even a name for this plan. It's called YRUU. And you wonder where all the young adults are.... [1]

Youth

For youth the question is not one of formal membership but of connection to the larger congregation.

For our discussion, youth are people under the age of eighteen. Some have parents who consider themselves Unitarian Universalists, while others don't. Most of these youth would self-identify as UUs, particularly those who have had several years of participation in an effective religious education program. For youth the question is not one of formal membership but of connection to the larger congregation. Are they just attendees at the church school, or are they recognized as members of the larger congregational community?

The questions are, "Has the religious education that youth have received helped prepare and motivate them for the step of affiliation and eventual membership?" "Are they moving along the path of maturational and incarnational growth?" "Do the curricula teach age-appropriate understandings of the meaning of membership in a UU congregation?" "Do they learn how the church really runs?" "About the relationship between this congregation and other UU congregations?" Sheri M. Prud'homme, a lifespan religious education consultant, says, "I have noticed that it tends to be easier for adults in their twenties and thirties who were not raised in the UU church to find homes in congregations. On some level, our youth ministries are not preparing our youth to be adult members of our congregations."[2]

Affiliation often begins with a child dedication ceremony in which an infant is accepted into the congregation. Some congregations have a ceremony that welcomes newly arrived older children into the congregation. These ceremonies are important recognitions of affiliation.

Especially for youth, affiliation often means connection at the district or continental level. This occurs for several reasons:

- As children grow, their horizons widen and they seek wider connections outside the congregation, just as they seek connections outside the home.
- Local congregations often don't have a large enough cohort of a narrow age range to form a viable group.
- District and continental programs are richer and more varied because they serve a larger group.
- There is often more adult support, including professional staff, at the district and national levels than at the local level.

These groups should be seen as opportunities to encourage youth's development of their UU identity.

Sometimes a congregation sees these connections as competitive, taking youth away. Instead, these groups should be seen as opportunities to encourage youth's development of their UU identity.

Children

The question of children becoming members is complex. Congregational practices vary widely, from no restrictions on youth membership to a minimum age requirement of eighteen. Why is there such a variety of practices?

- Because every congregation sets its own criteria for membership.
- Because the UUA makes no recommendations about age criteria for membership.
- Because it is mistakenly believed that minors can't be legal members.[3] (Congregations should check their state's or province's statutes to see whether there are restrictions on allowing minors to make financial decisions.)
- Because it is believed that youth cannot fulfill the obligations of membership.
- Because each congregation evolved its own practices differently.
- Because adults believe that children don't wish to become members.

When we asked youth about membership we received quite uniform opinions. Here is a typical example:

> I am seventeen years old and a member of Foothills Unitarian Church in Fort Collins, CO. The topic of youth membership is especially relevant to our church because in May the Congregational Meeting voted to approve a bylaw change concerning membership that was proposed by our youth group. Under the old bylaws, membership was restricted to those eighteen years or older. The new bylaws allow anyone to become a member, provided they go through a membership class or suitable substitute.... A membership class or other requirement of some kind gives the feeling (regardless of age) that membership is important and not something to be taken lightly.
>
> The bylaw change was passed almost unanimously, and we already have had seven youth (including myself) join the church. Although we won't be able to see the effects of this decision until the next congregational meeting this spring, I feel that our church is better off having made a statement that it values people regardless of age.

And another:

> I feel very strongly that no age should be imposed on membership because different people choose to become members at different times.... I feel that UU Principles compel our congregations to allow anyone who chooses to become a member to become a member.
>
> I really hope that your work encourages congregations to stop treating youth as second-rate UUs and when they become members to stop ignoring their potential to lead and actually teach adults quite a bit. For these reasons I would be against having a second category for youth membership; yes we are different but we don't need to be shut off any more from our faith. We want to be UUs and although we have different needs we try to meet them ourselves through YRUU and be active congregation members when we are given the chance.

If the requirements are well defined, we see no reason to have an arbitrary age limitation.

While we have no intention of infringing on the member congregations' right to set their own criteria for membership, we believe that considering the issue of youth membership will help congregations to clarify their views of the meaning of membership. If a congregation has established clear requirements for adult membership, it can then review those requirements to see how they can apply to youth. If the requirements are well defined, we see no reason to have an arbitrary age limitation. Young people will be able to meet the requirements at differing ages, depending on their maturity and congregation experience.

Many congregations have a Coming of Age program that marks the transition from childhood to youth. Participation in such a program might be recognized as equivalent to the new member classes given for adults. The completion of this program is a particularly appropriate time to invite youth to become members. It is a time when they are most connected and willing to consider joining. The argument that they are soon going to leave for college or other venues is specious. Youth need to be welcomed into the UU community, and this connection would encourage them to continue their UU affiliation as they move on.

Some congregations have established a special category of Youth Member. This may be just a way to avoid paying to the UUA's Annual Fund by not counting them as adult members. However, the UUA bylaws are clear that anyone who can vote is a member.[4] Of course, if the basis of the Fair Share contribution is changed this will cease to be a motivation.

Congregations need to value youth for their contributions, but not exploit them by just asking them to do tasks like baby sitting or dish washing. It is, for most congregations, *not* a good idea to have a designated seat for a youth on the board of trustees. If a youth is qualified and interested, he/she can be nominated and elected through the regular process. Too often, a designated youth is not sufficiently prepared or interested and soon drops away, not having had a good experience.

One of the questions that occurs for all ages, but particularly affects youth, is whether or not to have a minimum pledge amount. Here is one answer:

> If churches really understood and valued all of the contributions that they need to survive, these questions become a bit irrelevant. Anyone, regardless of age, ability, color, native tongue, or economic class can contribute something to the effective running of a church. This over-emphasis on money as a measure of commitment to church keeps youth and children from being able to be members, but it also throws off the balance of power in churches and is the birth of bad politics. (As in so-and-so has a little more say in the color of the sanctuary walls because so-and-so is paying to have them painted. And we all know that's the least of it.) Yes, I think all members should be canvassed every year to re-evaluate their pledge to the church. . . . A re-evaluation of this kind would not only take into consideration the new abilities, resources, and skills of the member, but give her a chance to remember what the church means to her, what it merits from her as a member.

One religious educator suggests,

> As a religious educator, the primary criterion I would use to determine whether an individual is old enough for congregational membership is whether the individual has reached Piaget's formal-operational stage of development (i.e., whether they can think abstractly). The formal-operational stage usually begins by about fourteen, but may come later. The bylaws of

Congregations need to value youth for their contributions, but not exploit them by just asking them to do tasks like baby sitting or dish washing.

the congregation I work for state that "any person who is at least sixteen years of age, or who has completed the ninth grade" may become a member. I feel this is a good practical statement of my primary criterion, since successful completion of the ninth grade typically calls for abstract thinking, and by age sixteen most persons in our culture have reached the formal-operational stage.

Young Adults

Young adults are defined by the UUA's Young Adult Ministries as age eighteen to thirty-five, but many of the older members are settled in their work and raising families. We therefore focus here on the younger of the young adults, age eighteen to twenty-five. This group is more likely to still be in school or in entry-level jobs. Why are they not found more often in our congregations? Sharon Hwang Colligan writes,

> At most congregations I visit, I look around the pews and see a sea of older faces. There are maybe three young adults there. But when time comes for visitors to stand and be greeted, two of the three young adults stand up. Clearly, they are not going to stay. *But they came*. And then at coffee hour, when I ask the elders why there are no young adults in the congregation, the answer I most often get is that "young adults are not interested in church." I think of all those young adult visitors, and I wonder what is not getting through.[5]

Young adults may come to identify as UUs by growing up in a UU congregation, or they may come as adults. They may find us through one of the many campus ministries at college, or they may connect through district or continental activities of the UU Young Adult/Campus Ministries Office. Frequently they are more involved with a district Young Adult group than with a local congregation. There are several reasons for this:

- Congregations, particularly smaller ones (and most of ours are smaller) may not have a large enough cohort of young adults to support specific programming for them.
- Congregations' programs are primarily directed to families and older adults, which constitute the majority of most congregations.
- Young adults are frequently in transition, changing their jobs, schools, and housing. Staying connected to a group in a larger area may be easier.
- The communications style of young adults, such as using electronic communications rather than mail, may be different from the traditional methods of our congregations.

- The leadership of congregations is mostly older, making it hard for young adults to relate to them. Young adults are not invited into leadership positions.

The question is then, "How do we encourage young adults to affiliate with and become members of our congregations?" This happens most frequently when they have children and bring them for religious education. Does your congregation do things like the following to connect it with young adults in the congregation?

- Support district young adult programs by offering the use of the congregation's facilities.
- Ask young adults what adult education programs would be of interest to them.
- Ask them when these programs should be offered. (They might not want to come at 9:00 on a Sunday morning.)
- Have older adults offer programs of interest to young adults either at the congregation or district levels. These might be on religious topics like ethics or theology or on more secular topics like writing skills.
- Invite young adults into leadership positions in the congregation. Actively recruit them, and then provide training and mentoring that will help them be effective. Although they are often busy, some do make time for volunteer activities. They often have special skills, like communications, finance, or publicity.
- Use contemporary music in the worship service, at least occasionally.
- Suggest to young adults in your congregation that when other young adults come to Sunday morning worship they invite the newcomers to join them for brunch afterward.
- Encourage your minister and lay leaders to meet with the young adult group in your congregation or district. Be clear that the ministry of the congregation is to young people as well as to older ones.
- Offer worship at other times as well as on Sunday morning. Young adults usually prefer a more informal and participative service, perhaps on a weekday evening.

Don't assume that all new members are new to Unitarian Universalism. Sheri M. Prud'homme says, "Simply put, if our congregation's worship life, educational programs, and spiritual practices cater to the New Unitarian Universalist, those who grew up Unitarian Universalist or those who have been members for over seven years will tend to look elsewhere for religious community."[6]

Our purpose here is not to present a description of a fully developed program but to indicate that action by congregations is needed if we want to have young adults affiliate.

Membership barriers for young adults (YA) are different from those of youth. Age requirements are not the problem. Their main problem is the lack of attention by the congregation to their needs and styles. Financial requirements can be a significant barrier. Donna DiSciullo, Young Adult/Campus Ministries director for the UUA says,

> With YAs being eighteen to thirty-five, you have a wide range of financial conditions. The younger group (eighteen to twenty-five) being the most transitory, financially strapped, low income. Others, especially the older YAs, don't want to be treated differently. At one GA, C*UUYAN[7] even sold buttons saying, "I'm a YA and I pledge." I do think there needs to be more work done on the part of congregations on getting YAs involved in the life of the congregation beyond the traditional child care and furniture moving—like invitations to sit on committees and boards—and leadership training to enhance those skills.

Here is one young adult's perspective on membership:

> I've never been able to put my finger on exactly what being a member (as opposed to a "friend") really means. OK, it means that one has voting privileges. It means a pledge is expected (as opposed to desirable). Of course one has certain privileges of use of church resources (fees for weddings are often reduced, for example)....Ultimately the obligation of being a member is to be a part of the collective whole. The privileges and any other obligations then are whatever the collective whole decides to award itself.

Here is another:

> I don't really feel that the "meaning" is different for me because I am a young adult. Key obligation: Contribute time and finances. Key privileges: Voting on issues. Officially part of the community.

Of course, not all young adults are without funds. Recently, a young member of one of our congregations received several million dollars when the company he worked for went public. If we stop focusing on the cost of membership in payments to the UUA and district, we may be able to pay more attention to the relationship of potential members.

The UUA has been expending a great effort toward becoming an anti-racist institution. Many of our young adults have a broader experience with people of color than our adults. This will be even more marked in the future as the multiracial children in our congregations mature. Here is one illustrative statement:

> One of the most important ideas I learned from communities of color is that ethnicity *matters*. UUs have a keen awareness of each individual's profound spiritual need to be unique, to express and be acknowledged for who you

Young adults' main problem is the lack of attention by the congregation to their needs and styles.

are. What UUs are less often able to perceive is that this spiritual need for uniqueness, to be who I am, extends into the collective or ethnic dimension.

I also learned that ethnicity is an especially strong part of young adult spiritual experience. Taking up the mantle of adulthood is taking up the legacy of the ancestors. Finding your calling as an adult is finding the way in which you will serve your people. If a young adult is not given an opportunity to reflect on this in a spiritual context, important developmental needs will not be met, and connections that could ground a person over a lifetime will not be made. The urgent young adult need to be a warrior, to serve, to lead, to make an impact on the world, risks being wasted in shallowness, misdirection, or despair.[8]

Campus Ministry

Campus ministry is different from young adult ministry. It takes place on college campuses but maintains a connection to a local congregation. Campus ministries have increased greatly over the past five years, due in large measure to the creation of a Young Adult/Campus Ministry staff at the UUA.

Campus ministries provide an *affiliation* for young adults, even if they are not members of a congregation. This affiliation maintains the contact that leads to future membership when the person moves to a new congregational community.

Why should congregations be interested in campus ministry? It is an outreach to young people that supports them in a transitional period in their lives and keeps them connected to Unitarian Universalism. It is both a service and an investment in the future, helping those served by providing a religious community and maintaining relationships with those who will become members of UU congregations later in life. In the past, some congregations marked the graduation from high school with a ceremony that essentially said "goodbye." More recently there has been a shift to a "bridging ceremony," which honors the change but emphasizes and encourages the continuing connection with Unitarian Universalism.

Why should congregations be interested in campus ministry? It is both a service and an investment in the future.

The connection can be maintained in many ways. You might see whether your congregation

- keeps young adults on the newsletter mailing list so they will know what is happening in their home congregation
- hosts a holiday gathering of young adults
- sends gift subscriptions to the *UU World* magazine or a college subscription to *Quest*, a publication of the Church of the Larger Fellowship
- sends HUUG's Baskets (see the YA/CM Information Packet) to new college students in their area

- offers rides to the congregation
- has a Host Homes program (connecting a UU student with a UU home)
- sponsors a campus ministry outreach program in your congregation

The bibliography lists many recently developed resources for both congregations and campus groups. They can easily be used if the congregation sees ministry to young adults on campus as an integral part of its outreach program.[9]

The Role of the Congregation

Congregations have a central role in keeping our youth and young adults connected with Unitarian Universalism. Sheri Prud'homme says, "There are at least three reasons we can't give up on the congregations. (1) Congregations carry our movement through time. They have proven to be flexible and enduring. (2) They are the embodiment of our values, providing the very real container in which we live out what we believe. (3) They provide critical mass through which we can act collectively."

The issue, then, is whether our congregations can see how important young people are to their future and whether the congregations can then adapt to the needs and interests of youth and young adults. We urge you to consider ways in which you can support young people in their relationships with your congregation and how you can encourage them to develop within our faith.

Congregations have a central role in keeping our youth and young adults connected with Unitarian Universalism.

Notes

1. Meg Muckenhoupt, "How to Kill a Religion," *Ferment: A Publication of the UU Young Adult/Campus Ministry Office* (Issue 13, January 2000): 6.
2. Sheri M. Prud'homme, Keynote address at ConCentric 2000 (Denton, MD, August 2000).
3. See Appendix B, "Legal Opinion on Youth Membership."
4. The "Members of Member Societies" section of the UUA bylaws states, "For the purposes of these Bylaws, a member of a member society is any individual who pursuant to its procedures has full or partial voting rights at business meetings of the society and who is certified as such by an authorized officer of the society" (Bylaws, Section C-3.11).
5. Sharon Hwang Colligan, "Children of the Same Tribe" (paper presented at UUA General Assembly, Nashville, TN, June 2000), 17. Visit www.circle maker.org/cdt.html to order copies.
6. Prud'homme, op. cit.

7. C*UUYAN Continental UU Young Adult Network. The community of young adults that encourages the formation, growth, and networking of UU young adult groups and provides leadership training and experience for young adults. C*UUYAN is a sponsored program of the UUA—hence its YA/CM program arm.
8. Colligan, op. cit.
9. All referenced resources can be reviewed and ordered on the UUA website at www.uua.org/ya-cm.
10. Prud'homme, op. cit.

Conclusion

In 1997, the Commission decided to study membership because the topic was important to our movement. Now, at the completion of our study, we are even more convinced of the significance this issue has for our liberal religious movement. We believe that a deeper and broader understanding of the meaning of membership is vital to our growth. The individual personal spiritual growth of each person who identifies with Unitarian Universalism and the growth of our congregations depend on deepening the theological understandings of membership and expanding the perspectives that are represented in our congregations. The challenges and opportunities abound.

A key concept underlying this report is our understanding of membership as a process. The theological perspective that grounds our work begins with St. Paul's classic metaphor of the relationship of the various "members" of the body and goes on to incorporate contemporary insights and ideas from many sources, liberation and process theology in particular. We chose our title, *Belonging*, near the end of our work, but it is central to Paul's original metaphor: Each organ of the body belongs to a whole that would not be whole without it. We find our wholeness in relationship, in community with others, people both like and unlike ourselves. Individually we are changed, transformed by our relationship with others; at the same time the community as a whole is changed by the presence and participation of each individual. Both individually and collectively we are in a constant state of change, of transformation. Transformation is the fundamental purpose of and reason for a religion

A deeper and broader understanding of the meaning of membership is vital to our growth.

of seriousness and depth. What we have called the process of membership is such a process, leading from superficial levels of identity and affiliation to deeper levels of commitment, to true membership.

We suggest three categories to outline this progression: *identification, affiliation,* and *membership*. The first is primarily self-identification: those who label themselves Unitarian Universalist but make no observable demonstration of their commitment—what someone has called "UUs without showing it." Affiliation implies some level of connection or participation in a congregation and/or other organizational involvement—for example, in youth programs, summer camps, or special interest groups. Membership suggests minimally an overt commitment, demonstrated by fulfilling stated institutional requirements, which is, however, only the beginning of a process of deepening participation and commitment, a process that may be lifelong. Again, our fundamental thesis is that membership is a process.

In this light we are asking our congregations to reconsider the meaning of membership and their practices relative to welcoming and incorporating new members. In our view all who participate in the life of a congregation are effectively members in some sense, whether or not they have signed the book or otherwise formalized their relationship. Practical considerations such as reporting requirements and denominational annual fund appeals based on Fair Share giving encourage a precision of definition that may be organizationally necessary but is essentially false. A congregation, any true community, is in an almost constant state of redefinition, based upon the complexities of the relationships and inter-relationships of which it is composed. At a given point in time the most influential member of a given congregation may not be technically a member at all but an individual whose behavior positively or negatively focuses the energy and direction of the whole.

Congregations, in other words, are also always involved in a process of transformation. They are different communities virtually every Sunday, affected by the changing needs and aspirations of their changing constituencies, those who are in the truest sense their members. A congregation that takes itself seriously, that takes its work seriously, will have a clear understanding of what its central purposes are, of what it is calling its members to. This is the basis of our claim that a study of membership is really a study about evangelism.

In order to build and sustain healthy congregations, we all have to work hard. Our questions of membership are directed at you, someone who has enough interest in our Unitarian Universalist faith to read this book. As a part of your own growth and development, we ask you to reach out to those who have not yet taken that step. In developing a new meaning of membership, we can better communicate what it means to be a Unitarian Universalist to others who are seeking. UUs must examine and clarify the concept of spiritual home and grapple with tough issues in creating it. The Commission calls you to ex-

A congregation that takes itself seriously will have a clear understanding of what it is calling its members to.

amine your own theology—your meaning making—and how that calls you to live your life. We challenge you, as we challenge ourselves, to think creatively about what UUs are called to be and do in the world. We ask you to invest yourself in your local congregation so that it and the more than one thousand like it provide healthy, nurturing, and challenging communities of faith—communities that are open to all who seek.

In the course of our study, we asked ourselves whether one can be a Unitarian Universalist without being a member of a congregation. We know that one's identification with Unitarian Universalism does not necessarily depend on membership in a UU congregation. While we believe that affiliation with a UU congregation is the most common way of strengthening that identification and deepening a personal theology, it is not the only way. Some have told us that congregation affiliation is difficult and painful. Therefore, it is in the best interests of our movement to honor and affirm those extra-congregational paths because they make it possible for many who would not otherwise be among us to remain. We call for congregations to look at the ways they exclude those with different voices so that all may find affiliation with a congregation deepening and meaningful.

We call on you to expand your thinking to get beyond numbers. Any discussion of membership that focuses only on numerical growth is incomplete. Not only are such assessments misleading but they consume time and energy that can be better used to build relationships and focus on common goals. In order for our congregations to be sources of strength, vitality, and vision we must pay attention to the quality of congregational life as well. Congregations are organic structures, reconstituting themselves with every person who joins or leaves them. If we do not view membership as being in continual formation and reformation, our congregations will become static and calcified. As Unitarian Universalists we must be continually challenged to reflect on our faith, on our relationship to congregations, to the Universalist movement, and on how our faith takes shape in the larger community. In doing so, the meaning of membership will be clarified and strengthened for each of us as individuals and for the congregations with which we affiliate.

Our congregations face particular challenges in carrying out the practices that we identify with deepening the meaning of membership. If we are to build an inclusive and dynamic theology of membership, we must live with the tension that comes from identifying common goals and interests at the same time that we welcome and incorporate differences. This is a creative tension that strengthens rather than diminishes our movement. In order to live our faith, we must understand and embrace practices and processes that overcome conflicts that inevitably arise in a dynamic, growing system.

In order to create healthy, open congregations, a systems perspective recommends an open discussion of norms and expectations of membership. Engaging in a discussion and clarification of the expectations of membership is what matters most. Avoiding that discussion results in ambiguity and ambivalence, which in turn create confusion, resentment, and alienation.

Our commitment to embracing diversity compels us to address the significant role that extra-congregational groups play in building the congregations that will, in turn, build a strong UU movement. Congregations are the foundation of our movement. They can and do provide support and community, especially in times of personal or spiritual crisis. Congregations can also become too comfortable. We get too comfortable thinking that everyone looks like us, believes as we do, and sees the world through the same cultural lenses. The result is a failure to live up to the theological basis of our free faith. We are called to listen to different voices and honor different experiences of the world. This call transcends tolerance. Indeed, tolerance is not enough. We are diminished individually and collectively if we fail to go beyond tolerance. We must celebrate and affirm the ways in which different experiences and perspectives enrich and strengthen our movement. The extra-congregational organizations discussed in this report play a vital role in helping us live our theology. They provide support and connection to many who do not yet feel included in a local congregation. They provide a beginning to important conversations. Such conversations are necessary if we are to truly learn and understand experiences of the world that are different from our own. Our congregational base does not mean we cannot find a broader understanding of how people come to identify with our movement and make stronger connections between our congregations and these important groups.

Youth and young adults present unique and important opportunities for they are the future of our movement. Most self-identify as Unitarian Universalist yet do not feel a connection to a local congregation. Many have participated in our religious education programs and are moving along that path of maturational and incarnational growth. All too often our congregations are not successful at engaging them in the life of the larger congregational community. We fail ourselves as well as our younger UUs when we overlook their contributions and their unique needs.

There are those who believe that we cannot survive the tension created by our efforts to address diversity. They call for us to emphasize what we have in common, minimizing the differences. This is not our conclusion. Rather, we believe that choosing to live in this tension will help our movement grow, not only numerically but in all respects. Our world cries out for a vision of different religions, different cultures, and different traditions living in harmony. We believe our faith community offers such a vision.

We acknowledge a risk in engaging in the kinds of discussions we propose. We have raised provocative questions that will foster discussion around the continent—questions that may well introduce difference of opinion into the daily life of our congregations. Bringing a discussion of norms and expectations into the open raises the likelihood of conflict. How congregations deal with these conflicts has a significant impact on membership and is an important dimension of organic growth.

We believe that we are up to the challenge. We encourage you to act on our recommendations. Most of all, we ask you to deepen your commitment to growth, your own and that of your congregation. Together we will all reach new experiences of belonging and an enhanced understanding of the meaning of membership.

The Epiphany Covenant

Our common covenant:

In the love of truth and the spirit of Jesus Christ, we unite for the worship of God and the service of humanity.

I own this covenant by...

committing to my own integrity. I fearlessly *seek the truth* of my life. I reflect on my beliefs and actions and take responsibility for my spiritual growth.

committing to be open to the *spirit of Jesus Christ*. I make his life and teachings my guide. As he loved God and neighbor, so I strive to love ever more fully. Especially, I love and learn from people of different religions and backgrounds, recognizing—as Jesus taught—that all people are loved by God.

committing to the health of this congregation. *We unite* by giving of ourselves to the tasks we choose together. I commit to give to my greatest capability and learn to discern my human limitations, that I may be a cheerful giver.

committing to the worship of God. I honor the presence of the divine in my life, that my relationship with God may grow. I am faithful in our common worship, recognizing that there is a strength in coming together which I cannot find alone.

---

committing to the service of humanity. As God works through me, I become a servant of the greater good.

That you may keep this covenant in faithfulness, Epiphany Community Church...

commits to providing opportunities for truth-seeking. Worship, classes, book studies, and discussion groups are available.

commits to providing opportunities for building community. In small groups, over time, authentic love develops. You are encouraged to join one.

commits to fair and just stewardship of resources. Your giving, whether of time or of money, will serve the greater mission of the church.

commits to providing regular worship opportunities. We grow with God every Sunday and whenever we gather.

commits to providing ways and means for you to find your particular "path of service." Leadership opportunities, workshops, and service projects are readily available.

—Epiphany Community Church, Fenton, Michigan

UUA Corporate Counsel Opinion on Membership

June 8, 2001

Ms. Kathleen C. Montgomery
Executive Vice President
Unitarian Universalist Association
25 Beacon Street
Boston, MA 02108

Re: *Unitarian Universalist Association—Board of Trustees*

Dear Kay:

At your request, here is our opinion concerning whether a minor may serve on (1) the Board of Trustees of the Unitarian Universalist Association, a Massachusetts non-profit corporation organized under Chapter 180 of the General Laws, or (2) the governing board of a member congregation.

In rendering this opinion, we examined such documents and made such other investigations as we deemed appropriate. The opinion is limited to Massachusetts law.

In short, there is nothing in Massachusetts law that prohibits a minor from serving as a board member, director, trustee or officer. While Section 3 of Chapter 180 provides that: "One or more persons, of the age of eighteen years or more in the case of natural persons, may act as incorporators to form a corporation...," there is no similar age restriction for corporate directors, trustees or officers.

A non-profit corporation or association may prescribe in its Articles of Organization or bylaws a minimum age and other qualifications of its directors, trustees and officers. Absent a restriction, however, a minor is not disqualified from serving. The UUA's bylaws do not preclude a minor from serving as trustee.

Congregations organized under the laws of states other than Massachusetts will need to check the applicable laws of their states, as well as their Articles of Organization and bylaws.

Very truly yours,

Edward P. Leibensperger

Resources

Alexander, Scott W. ed. *Salted With Fire: UU Strategies for Sharing Faith and Growing Congregations*. Boston: Skinner House Books, 1994.

A collection of voices inspired with enthusiasm for championing the cause of our liberal faith. UU leaders from our own local communities discuss historical and modern interpretations of UU evangelism and offer ideas and practical advice for congregational growth.

Barber, Benjamin R. *A Place for Us: How to Make Society Civil and Democracy Strong*. New York: Hill and Wang, 1998.

Benjamin Barber attempts to retrieve the ideals of "civil society" from those who want to re-create old-fashioned (and discriminatory) small communities and from the free-marketeers who associate it with unfettered commercial activity. The book offers strategies for civilizing public discourse and promoting civic debate.

Beard, Margaret L., and Roger W. Comstock, eds. *All Are Chosen; Stories of Lay Ministry and Leadership*. Boston: Skinner House Books, 1998.

These are first-person accounts of people who have become deeply involved in various aspects of UU life as lay leaders. They range from brand new churches to New England "churches on the green," from campus ministries to worship associates. There are some very eloquent descriptions of lay ministries: worship associates, pastoral associates, social justice, and youth ministries, etc. Especially recommended are the essays by Beverly Smrha ("Congregations as Seminary for the Laity"—using Roy Phillips's language), Mary Ella Holst ("Social Justice as Lay Ministry"—makes the distinction between a volunteer and a lay minister), Laila D. Ibrahim ("Paul Just Died"—incredibly eloquent), Roger Comstock ("Ministry to Each Other Comes First"—talks about membership as a covenant).

Callahan, Kennon. *Twelve Keys to an Effective Church: Strategic Planning for Mission*. San Francisco: HarperSanFrancisco, 1983.

This oldie-but-goodie identifies the essential characteristics of an effective, growing, healthy congregation and suggests ways to develop each of them. Not all of the chapters will be relevant to Unitarian Universalist congregations. For instance, the chapter on pastoral and lay visitation is probably one you will want to skip. But the section "Significant Relational Groups" is particularly relevant, as are the sections "Specific, Concrete Missional Objectives," "Strong Leadership Resources," and "Streamlined Structure and Solid, Participatory Decision Making."

Continental Unitarian Universalist Young Adult Network website: www.uuyan.org.

Links to information about programs for young adults, including district groups and resources.

Emerson, Dorothy May, ed. *Standing Before Us: Unitarian Universalist Women and Social Reform, 1776–1936*. Boston: Skinner House Books, 1999.

This anthology includes writings by, and biographical sketches of, fifty Universalist and Unitarian women. The four sections—"Call to Reform," "Search for Education," "Struggle for Racial Justice," and "Reform in Religion"—demonstrate the impact of women's leadership in creating significant social change.

Essex Conversations Coordinating Committee. *Essex Conversations: Visions for Lifespan Religious Education*. Boston: Skinner House Books, 2001.

As Unitarian Universalists enter the twenty-first century, what is central for our evolving faith? What are our goals for lifespan religous education? What are the vital components for our curricula?

Foster, Charles R. *Embracing Diversity: Leadership in Multicultural Congregations*. Washington, DC: Alban Institute, 1997.

Explores a variety of approaches congregations have taken to embrace differences, identify leadership issues diversity creates in congregations, and discover programmatic suggestions drawn from the experience of multicultural congregations to address these issues.

Foster, Charles R., and Theodore Brelsford. *We Are the Church Together: Cultural Diversity in Congregational Life.* Valley Forge, PA: Trinity Press, 1996.

> On-the-scene research in three culturally diverse congregations in a large Southern city addresses what it means to be "church" in a culturally diverse congregation. The authors call for a radical rethinking and reconfiguration of conventional theological, educational, and polity assumptions.

Friedman, Edwin. *Generation to Generation: Family Process in Church and Synagogue.* New York: Guilford Press, 1985.

> This classic text applies systems theory to congregational life. Much of the material in this book is the underlying basis for assumptions in this report about the way congregations function as organic entities. Friedman's discussion of the nature of healthy leadership in a system is particularly helpful.

Heller, Anne Odin. *Churchworks: A Well-Body Book for Congregations.* Boston: Skinner House Books, 1999.

> Covers all vital congregational concerns—spiritual development, growth and new membership, conflict resolution, lay and professional ministry, building and grounds, congregational structure, and fundraising.

Hertz, Walter P., ed. *Redeeming Time: Endowing Your Church with the Power of Covenant.* Boston: Skinner House Books, 1998.

> Resource for congregations to renew their foundational promise for support and accountability in our liberal religious community. Includes sample covenants and discussion questions.

Kirkpatrick, Thomas. *Small Groups in the Church: A Handbook for Creating Community.* Washington, DC: Alban Institute, 1995.

> Kirkpatrick begins by talking about the challenge of creating community in our contemporary culture. He then offers some specific guidelines for planning small-group ministry, training leaders and facilitators, and sustaining small groups in the congregation.

Lavanhar, Marlin. "Soulful Sundown: a Manual." Boston: Young Adult/Campus Ministry Office, UUA, 1999. Available at www.uua.org/ya.com.

> A new contemporary UU worship style for young adults that explores the arts and spirituality through the interaction of local and national artists—i.e., blues, jazz, and folk performers; storytellers; comedians; dancers; and other artists with UU worship leaders. A new resource for young adult worship. This manual will help you re-create the successful Soulful Sundown worship experience in your congregation or district.

Mann, Alice. *The In-Between Church: Navigating Size Transitions in Congregations*. Washington, DC: Alban Institute, 1998.

Mann's book is a good resource for congregational leaders who are feeling the tension and frustration of being in size transitions. She offers a good framework for understanding how people in churches experience growth and change and suggests ways that these transitions can be navigated in good faith by the leadership and the membership.

Mead, Loren B. *More Than Numbers: The Way Churches Grow*. Washington, DC: Alban Institute, 1993.

This book has informed the growth strategies of many of the new and growing congregations in the UUA. Mead builds on the work of Ted Buckle in suggesting that there are four distinct dynamics to church growth: numerical growth, maturational growth, organic growth, and incarnational growth. In the context of Mead's model, growth is understood to be a complex and multifaceted phenomenon that is inseparable from the meaning of membership.

Oswald, Roy M. *Assimilating New Members: The Workshop*. Washington, DC: Alban Institute, 1990. Videocassettes.

Based on Alban and other studies that led to the book *The Inviting Church* (see below), these tapes identify the common characteristics of congregations that are warm, inviting, and growing. Taped by sponsoring church in VHS format, runs about four hours on two tapes. Includes a Discussion Leader's Guide.

Oswald, Roy M., and Speed B. Leas. *The Inviting Church: A Study of New Member Assimilation*. Washington, DC: Alban Institute, 1987.

Although somewhat old and not specifically UU, this is one of the standard guides to membership. Ever wonder why some people never return after their first visit? Why some join but you rarely see them? Or why others become active participants in your church family's life and worship? Discover how your congregation can meet growth challenges. Based on Alban Institute research, *The Inviting Church* includes a self-study design for assessing assimilation processes and analyzing visitors' perceptions.

Parsons, George, and Speed Leas. *Understanding Your Congregation as a System: The Manual*. Washington, DC: Alban Institute, 1993.

This book provides a short and accessible course in the basics of congregational systems theory. Vocabulary, concepts, real-world examples—they're all here.

Phillips, Roy. *Transforming Liberal Congregations for the New Millennium.* St. Paul, MN: Unity Church—Unitarian, 1996.

This book actually began as the 1995 Minns Lectures. Phillips's premise is that we need new models for growing and sustaining liberal congregations in order to keep our movement healthy and vital. He draws extensively on a number of well-known writers in contemporary congregational life (Kennon Callahan, Loren Mead, Parker Palmer). His theological underpinnings come from the nineteenth-century Transcendentalists and from the more recent work of Henry Nelson Wieman.

Phillips, Roy D. *Letting Go: Transforming Congregations for Ministry.* Washington, DC: Alban Institute, 1999.

This is a slightly revised version of *Transforming Liberal Congregations for the New Millennium* and is easier to acquire. Pioneering thinkers have been saying for decades that the key to church renewal lies in nurturing the ministry of the laity. Based on his thirty-plus years of experience in parish ministry, Phillips makes the case that in order for lay ministries to flourish, pastors need to let go of their traditional views about their role in the congregation. *Letting Go* forthrightly explains what it means for pastors to do less so their members have the opportunity and freedom to grow. Foreword author Michael Cowan promises, "Pastors and lay leaders approaching this book with practical hopes, needs, and questions will not be disappointed."

Rendle, Gilbert. *Leading Change in the Congregation: Spiritual and Organizational Tools for Leaders.* Washington, DC: Alban Institute, 1998.

A well-written book about how congregational leaders can help their organizations to get "unstuck" and to embrace change as a welcome and healthy way to grow. It includes lots of short exercises for church leaders who want to understand where their congregations are, what is keeping them there, and what can help them to get moving again.

Southworth, Bruce. *At Home in Creativity: The Naturalistic Theology of Henry Nelson Wieman.* Boston: Skinner House Books, 1995.

Wieman is a process philosopher and theologian. His writing is often complex and hard to penetrate; the vocabulary of process theology is obscure to most of us. Bruce Southworth has done a good job of explaining and translating him. The core of Wieman's theology is his understanding of God as the creative event—creative interchange as God operating in human history. Southworth summarizes this complicated philosophy: "Wieman's philosophical and theological goal responded to the question, 'How do we know/experience God?' The answer: In creativity. Simultaneously he was asking, 'How might we be saved?' The answer: By faith—by ultimate commitment to God, which is commitment to the Creative Process, a commitment that necessitates our co-creativity."

Steinke, Peter L. *Healthy Congregations: A Systems Approach*. Washington, DC: Alban Institute, 1996.

> Steinke offers ten principles of health in a congregation, beginning with "wholeness is not attainable, but it can be approximated." A reassuring and easy-to-read book that covers the basics of congregational systems theory, including chapters on anxiety and fear of change preventing rather than resolving serious conflicts over growth.

Trumbauer, Jean Morris. *Sharing the Ministry: A Practical Guide for Transforming Volunteers Into Ministers*. Minneapolis, MN: Augsburg Fortress Publishers, 1995.

> Helps congregations look at their members in terms of providing them with "ministries" in the church and the surrounding community.

Trumbauer, Jean Morris. *Created and Called: Discovering Our Gifts for Abundant Living*. Minneapolis, MN: Augsburg Fortress Publishers, 1999.

> Explores the interrelationship between God's creation and us, as well as the mission and ministry we do both as individuals and as communities of faith.

Unitarian Universalist Association. *InterConnections*. Published five times per year.

> This small newsletter is sent to the lay leadership of each congregation and is available on the web at www.uua.org/interconnections. There is a searchable InterConnections Resource Library at this web address. Vol II, Issue V, contains an index of articles in the first two volumes. See particularly Vol II, Issue V, for the article on small groups, and Vol III, Issue IV, for articles on newcomer classes and encouraging youth involvement.

Weeks, Andrew D. *Welcome! Tools and Techniques for New Member Ministry*. Washington, DC: Alban Institute, 1992.

> This toolkit of intentional and compassionate strategies takes an encouraging, incremental approach to help even small groups get started quickly. Adapt an additional thirty-four pages of template forms, brochures, and procedures to your needs while employing Weeks's point-by-point recommendations to make sure your signs and property invite, not confuse; create powerful, welcoming ads and print communication; train and prepare greeters; develop programs to incorporate and track newcomers during their critical first three, six, nine, and twelve months.

Wells, Barbara, and Jaco B. ten Hove. *Articulating (Y)Our Faith: A Creative Way to Explore and Express the Basics of UUism*. Boston: Young Adult/Campus Ministry Office, UUA, 2000. Available at www.uua.org/ya.com.

Responding to the complaints they have heard throughout their ministry about how difficult it is to describe UUism, Barbara and Jaco designed this workshop Leader's Guide (with an Addendum of Resources). They have found creative ways to encourage folks over the hurdles that keep them from expressing their UU faith to others. While written with young adults in mind, it can be productively adapted and used by all generations.

Young Adult/Campus Ministry Office. "Bridging Ceremony Resource Packet." Boston: UUA, 1997. Available at www.uua.org/ya-cm.

A packet of materials to assist you in changing your traditional end-of-year CLIFF ceremony to a BRIDGING ceremony, a ceremony that recognizes the important transition from youth to young adulthood. It includes a history, sample orders of service, readings and suggestions, testimonies, and ideas for staying connected to your young people after high school.

Young adult annotated resource list: www.uua.org/ya.

This web page has a wealth of information about a variety of publications for creating and sustaining programs for young adults. It also has links to some web sources.

Young Religious Unitarian Universalists (YRUU) resource list: www.uua.org/YRUU/resources.html.

See "The Five Components of a Balanced Youth Program" for descriptions of worship, community building, social action, learning, and leadership.